S0-EAW-539

Rudolf Jaeger, Editor

Grilling
Like a Champion

4880 Lower Valley Road • Atglen, PA 19310

Copyright © 2014 by Schiffer Publishing Ltd.

Library of Congress Control Number: 2014933564

All rights reserved. No part of this work may be reproduced or used in any form or by any means—graphic, electronic, or mechanical, including photocopying or information storage and retrieval systems—without written permission from the publisher.

The scanning, uploading, and distribution of this book or any part thereof via the Internet or via any other means without the permission of the publisher is illegal and punishable by law. Please purchase only authorized editions and do not participate in or encourage the electronic piracy of copyrighted materials.
"Schiffer," "Schiffer Publishing, Ltd. & Design," and the "Design of pen and inkwell" are registered trademarks of Schiffer Publishing, Ltd.

ISBN: 978-0-7643-4498-5
Printed in China

Published by Schiffer Publishing, Ltd.
4880 Lower Valley Road
Atglen, PA 19310
Phone: (610) 593-1777; Fax: (610) 593-2002
E-mail: Info@schifferbooks.com

For our complete selection of fine books on this and related subjects, please visit our website at www.schifferbooks.com. You may also write for a free catalog.

This book may be purchased from the publisher. Please try your bookstore first.

We are always looking for people to write books on new and related subjects. If you have an idea for a book, please contact us at proposals@schifferbooks.com.

Schiffer Publishing's titles are available at special discounts for bulk purchases for sales promotions or premiums. Special editions, including personalized covers, corporate imprints, and excerpts can be created in large quantities for special needs. For more information, contact the publisher.

Originally published © 2010 by HEEL Verlag GmbH under the title Grillen wie die Weltmeister. Translated by Christine Marie Elliston

This cook book was written according to best knowledge and belief. Neither the publisher nor the editor are responsible for unintended reactions or damage that result from working with the ingredients. No responsibility is accepted for the correctness of this information.

Foreword

When the first rays of sun force their way through the clouds in the spring, you set your grill in the garden or on the terrace again. The charcoal doesn't want to light, you try all types of remedies, but the ancient grill doesn't draw properly and is shaky. With anticipation, already marinated, purchased pork bellies and pork neck steaks are placed on the grill, the kids quickly get a couple of sausages beforehand. It's fun for the first one or two times, but then a few family members turn their noses up and demand change. You are also no longer content and look forward to new ideas. Does this sound familiar to you?

We would like to provide you with support at this point and give you ideas on how to simply prepare refined dishes on the grill that will please you, your family, and your guests.

In addition to 124 recipes, the introductory section of this book on theory presents information on different possibilities, with which devices you can prepare and grill food on an open fire, and gives you all kinds of tips and tricks that will make even the greatest trivial pursuit in the world easy for you. Additionally, you will receive information on individual types of meat and fish, their preparation, and much more.

This book is for beginners as well as advanced learners. The steps for preparation are described clearly, and the recipes are accompanied by many photographs. It is also important for us that the ingredients are easy to obtain and that the dishes are easy to duplicate. We have tested all of the recipes. You can be certain that nothing will go wrong during preparation. Even professional grillers will enjoy the elaborate instructions and definitely find a tip or two that they can use.

Your guests will thank you!

Contents

PART 2 - The Recipes   84

PART 3 - Appendix   221

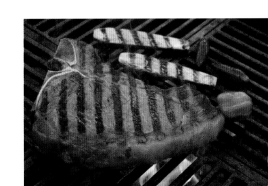

1. Different Grilling Methods

Direct Grilling:
320-575°F (160-300°C)

For this direct method, the food is placed directly onto the grate over lit charcoal and heated. So that both sides are cooked, it must be turned over after half of the cooking time. This method is suitable for steaks, hamburgers, cutlets, and other food with short cooking times.

Cooking time: Up to 25 minutes

Indirect Grilling:
320-400°F (160-200°C)

Here the meat is not cooked over a heat source, but rather by smoke and warm air. The food does not lie over the heat source but usually over a drip pan that can be filled with liquid. The fuel is piled up next to the drip pan — the term "indirect" grilling stems from this. Of course, it takes longer than direct grilling, but the meat becomes as soft as butter and very tender. The indirect grilling method is similar to slow cooking, but the food is grilled and from this possesses a better flavor and look than you can achieve in an oven. The rising heat, reflected by the lid and the inner surface of the grill, cooks the food evenly on all sides. The circulating heat works like a convection oven, which is why the food must not be turned over.

This method is especially suitable for food that must be grilled for longer than 25 minutes or is too sensitive to be cooked using the direct grilling method, because otherwise it would dry out or burn: for example, roasts, ribs, whole chickens, turkey, other large pieces of meat, or fish fillets. This is especially true with raw sausages, which can, indirectly, be brought to the correct temperature so that they do not burn too quickly with direct heat that is too high. In the last several minutes, they are grilled directly so that they turn a nice color.

Cooking time: 25 minutes to 5 hours depending on size and temperature

Barbecuing:
190-320°F (90-160°C)

Here the fire is in the side firebox, and the delicacies cook at a low temperature. Preferably use fruit tree wood. Leave the firebox lid open a small gap, and the result will be incredible: no dryness, no grease fire, and no turning. You will get food with a lot of flavor and enormous juiciness.

Cooking time: From 3 hours on

Steaming:
140-200°F (60-90°C)

Smoking:
200-250°F (90-120°C)

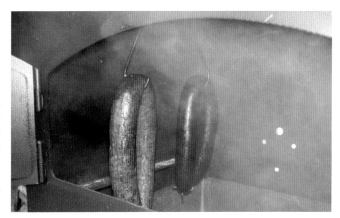

The heat source is used in the same way as barbecuing, but the ventilation flaps are closed, and a strong smoke develops. By selecting the type of wood, you can determine the smoke intensity and flavor. The right smoker does well in a garden.

Cooking time: You need patience here — up to 24 hours!

Cold Smoking

Cold smoking occurs at temperatures from 60–80°F (15-26°C) with special hardwoods. Food that should be made to last longer, such as sausage, ham, or bacon, are cold smoked. Cold smoking is a process that takes several days and is done in a smokehouse. Because no cooking process takes place here, the smoking does not affect the inner structure of the meat. This grilling method is mostly combined with the salting of smoked food.

Spin Grilling

A special grilling method from Saarland using charcoal and a spin grill with a tripod.

Plank Grilling

Plank grilling is a method that was invented by the native inhabitants of America. Here fish, meat, or vegetables are cooked on a wooden board. While cooking, the food absorbs some of the flavor from the wood, and the smoke of the charred wood passes its flavor to the food.

Dutch Oven

A Dutch oven is a thick-walled, cast iron cooking pot with a tight-fitting lid. The functionality of a Dutch oven is simple. Charcoal is placed underneath the pot and on the lid, and the heat is transferred to the cast iron. Here a large portion of the heat should come from above because the cast iron distributes the heat evenly over the entire pot and gently cooks the food without burning. Because of the weight of the lid, a Dutch oven basically works like a pressure cooker.

If you consistently take care of the Dutch oven from the start, then it will last for many years.

Wood-Fired Oven ⎯⎯⎯⎯

Baking with a wood-fired oven is a very primordial type of food preparation. You can grill, braise, bake, gratinate, and smoke in it. The special taste experience that people in the age of industrial mass production miss more and more is achieved with the incomparable wood-fired oven flavor. The radiant heat from the stones combined with the unique scent of the wood fire give the baked goods an extraordinary flavor that cannot be obtained in an oven in which the baking chamber and combustion chamber are separated from each other.

The functionality and operation of the ovens are simple and ingenious. In the combustion chamber, you light thinly split wood, bring the oven to the right temperature, maintain the heat, and bake your dish with the radiant heat of the stones and with the heat of the fire in the combustion chamber.

You bake dishes, such as bread or meat, either continually with constant low heat or heat up the combustion chamber and bake with decreasing heat. This not only helps you to achieve the natural, savory flavor of the individual dish, but it will also create a cozy ambience in conjunction with an original baking experience.

A Few Suggestions

- Before grilling, fan away the ashes. Caution: Flying sparks!

- Before grilling lean meat or fish, oil the grate (or the grill food) to prevent sticking.

- When turning over the meat, don't become too inpatient. It's mostly sufficient to turn the pieces of meat only once; in particular this gives the meat a nice branding.

- Always use stable tongs to turn the meat, so you do not perforate the meat and you won't drop a piece on the floor.

- Never grill too many pieces at once. If the meat stays on the grill too long and no one eats it, the meat will quickly become dry and tough.

- Season with salt only after grilling, especially steaks.

- Let especially beef rest for at least five minutes after grilling to increase the spreading of the meat juices. The meat then remains juicy and incredibly tender.

- Always cut shortly grilled products diagonally against the grain.

- Do not place cured meat on the grill. Such types of meat are treated with nitrite curing salt to preserve it longer. With high heat, the nitrite from the salt can react with special proteins, amines, from the meat. As a result, nitrosamines develop, which are hazardous to your health.

- Create different temperature zones on the grill by varying the distribution of the charcoal. You can "park" the meat in warm zones shortly before eating.

- You should absolutely avoid cutting the meat while grilling. Not only does it lose some juiciness from this, but the escaping liquid also causes the heat source to go up in flames.

- Fish should not remain on the grill too long, otherwise it will become dry. When the fish is white and opaque, but at the same time moist and juicy, and as soon as you can pull it apart with a fork, the fish is done.

- Pork and poultry should always be served well done.

- Beef can be cooked rare, medium, and well done according to taste.

- If you use sugar or honey in marinades, you should coat the food only during the last few minutes or work with medium heat. Otherwise the sugar becomes too dark.

Tip

For flat grill food, you can use the hand test to determine its doneness: the longer the meat is cooked, the firmer it is. If it feels soft, then it is still raw inside. If the meat is springy when you press on it, the inside is pink or medium. It is firm when well done.

Simple rule of thumb: Touch the fingertip of your middle finger (ring finger or pinky finger) with your thumb on one hand (don't press) and with a finger on your other hand press on the area between your wrist and the base of your thumb. You simply test how soft the area between your wrist and thumb, or steak, is. The following rules apply:

Thumb and middle finger: rare
Thumb and ring finger: medium
Thumb and pinky finger: well done

Important: You can enjoy beef and lamb medium or rare, but pork, chicken, and turkey should be well done.

Cleaning the Grate

There are many possibilities here. You can, for example, leave the grate on the grill after grilling — wait until the charcoal has gone out and then simply scrape off the rest with a steel wool pad. If you would you like to help your stainless steel grate reach its full glory, then clean it with dish soap and a steel wool pad over the sink. However, don't forget to rub your cast iron grate with neutral vegetable oil before putting it back into the grill because otherwise it will rust all too easily.

The grill food cooks internally from heat conduction. The outer layers slowly give their heat inward. Thus, flat pieces only need a short amount of time and high heat. At high heat, large roasts would become charred on the outside and remain raw inside. You need medium, long-lasting heat that can slowly penetrate inside. Therefore, consider the sequence with which you apply the food: small sausages need less time than, for example, spare ribs that must be grilled slowly and carefully.

2. Types of Grills

Charcoal Grill

Quaint, romantic, but also costly. The charcoal needs at least a half hour until the grilling fun can begin. Charcoal grills are available in different sizes, materials, and designs. Depending on the location, a device made of enameled steel is recommended because it is weatherproof.

How it's done

If you do not have a charcoal starter, then layer the charcoal into a pile and light it. As soon as a fine, light gray ash layer has formed on the charcoal (after at least 25 minutes), then it can begin. Devices that have their own charcoal grate allow more oxygen to reach the charcoal, and the heat generation is stronger.

Advantages:

■ Charcoal gives the grill food the typical grill flavor.

■ A charcoal grill is more favorable than comparable gas grills and universally usable because neither gas cylinders nor an electrical connection is necessary.

■ The only true grilling method for many grillers.

Disadvantages:

■ The smoke and odor can irritate sensitive neighbors.

■ Charcoal grills are sensitive to wind, and the ashes can swirl up and settle on the grill food.

■ When grease drips on the heat source, harmful substances are formed — so-called benzopyrene and nitrosamine.

Gas Grill

Gas grills are operated with liquid gas, such as butane or propane. It is easier to grill with a gas grill instead of a charcoal grill because it does not take long for gas grills to heat up. Unfortunately, gas grills are technically more demanding and are more liable to break down. Approximately thirty percent of all grilling devices are operated with gas.

The Different Types of Devices

On many devices there are lava stones or ceramic briquettes under the grate that are heated. They are very porous and because of this can absorb large amounts of dripping grease. Thus, hardly any harmful substances are formed. However, you should make sure that a water pan is underneath the stones to catch the grease. Side burners are ideal here: darting flames do not form in the center of the grill when something drips down.

Other devices have gas flames under angle bars made of enameled steel or cast iron plates that are heated by burners.

Large rectangular gas grills have lids and multiple burners that can be lit separately, which allows for direct and indirect grilling. In addition, you can set different temperature zones with more grates, which allows simultaneous cooking of different dishes. The aromatization of the grill food is easy to manage: place soaked (at least 30 minutes, preferably 2 hours) wood chips in aluminum foil and poke a few holes in it with a fork. Expose this pack to direct heat, close the lid, and it is already emitting its fragrance and flavor that settles on the grill food.

Gas grills are often offered completely in grill carts. From this, you get additional warming racks, cabinets, removable working surfaces, folding tables, cutlery holders, and much more.

Important Factors When Buying a Gas Grill

When buying a gas grill and accessories, such as hose lines and pressure regulators, take advice from knowledgeable sales staff and familiarize yourself with the operation of the device. When making a new purchase, make sure that a certification mark is affixed to the gas grill or on the attached data plate and that an operation manual is enclosed. It also applies here: more electricity voltage = more power.

> **Safety Note:**
>
> When buying a gas grill, you should absolutely make sure it has been ceritified for safety. Among the reputable certifying agences are UL, Intertek Testing, NSF, and CSA. They insist that their certification label is placed on the grill in plain sight. If you don't see it, the certification is not valid.

You reach high temperatures with gas. However, the heat on round grill plates is not evenly distributed. The highest heat is directly over the burner ring; towards the center and edge, it clearly decreases. Many burners do not produce a nice ring of flames at all, but rather flicker back and forth. It is best to first check the device of your choice.

Things to Consider When Setting Up and Operating Gas Grills

■ Before you use the gas grill for the first time, carefully read the operating instructions and especially the safety tips and instructions on connecting the liquid gas cylinder, and pay attention to the setup and operation of the device.

■ Use the gas grill only outdoors, and set up in a well-ventilated area and at a sufficient distance from flammable materials and low-lying areas, manholes, or drains.

■ Make sure that the liquid gas cylinder is operated only when standing upright and is set up far away from sources of heat.

■ Connect the gas grill only with a pressure regulator and an appropriate hose line; the length should not exceed five feet (1.50m), with the cylinder valve. Note the left-handed thread!

■ There is a large number of different manufacturers — research the different brands online if need be. Some of the brands are: Outdoorchef, Weber, Napoleon, Grandhall, Santos.

Tip!

You should always have at least one gas cylinder on reserve!

Advantages: ──────────────

■ The gas grill is very easy to start with an automatic (electronic) ignition.

■ Gas grills have a minimal preheating time.

■ The heat can be adjusted variably with a control knob.

■ Gas grills are easier to clean than charcoal grills.

■ Gas grills produce hardly any smoke.

■ The grill can be used on a balcony.

Disadvantages: ──────────────

■ Gas grills are very heavy, bulky, and correspondingly difficult to transport.

■ The grill food does not have the typical charcoal grill flavor.

■ You always need a full gas cylinder.

■ With many models, the grease accumulates under the stones. Not only is It difficult to remove, but it also drips on the burners.

■ Due to the greater technical demands, gas grills are more expensive than charcoal grills.

Kettle Grill ———————————

In 1952, George Stephen invented the first kettle grill in Chicago. He was fed up with the constantly dripping grease causing the charcoal to burn and searched for a different option to gently cook large roasts and pieces of meat. Because he worked in a metal factory that manufactured buoys, he took this shape as an example and constructed the first kettle grill. All kettle grills basically consist of two halves that are nearly the same size. The charcoal grate lies in the lower half, the fuel does not lie directly on the base of the lower chamber. From the ventilation system, the charcoal receives more oxygen from below and, thus, produces a consistent heat more quickly. The stainless steel grate that is mostly not height-adjustable is located over it.

The top, removable half has a handle, ventilation holes, and also a thermometer on most models. The kettle grill stands on three legs, two of which are mostly equipped with wheels. The devices are much easier to place in the garden, and they do not wobble on any surface.

The meat is not cooked over the heat source here, but rather indirectly from the smoke and the warm air. You will find more information on indirect grilling on page 8.

Advantages: ———————————

■ The charcoal cannot be ignited by dripping grease.

■ Even large food, like roasts, chickens, duck, and much more, can be prepared.

■ No grease reaches the heat source, and no harmful substances are formed.

■ The meat won't burn as easily, becomes tender, and gets a small pink smoke edge.

Because the kettle grill is naturally not made from transparent materials there is no view of the grill food. In order to not constantly open the lid, which means prolonging the cooking time due to the escaping heat, you can use a practical aid like a temperature probe. With this you have complete control over the core temperature of the roast and can cook it to perfection.

If you additionally want more smoky flavor you can easily place soaked wood chips on the charcoal. Depending on the type of wood, these then give the grill food their flavors.

Important Factors When Buying a Kettle Grill

Kettle grills are available in multiple sizes. The diameter of the models ranges between 11-3/4" (30cm) and almost three feet (1m). When making a purchase, this should be the most important criteria. Naturally, you can also wonderfully directly grill with all models. Here a version with 11-3/4" (30cm) is sufficient for most. A diameter of 22-1/2" (57cm) initially seems somewhat too big for most. However, you should consider that with larger diameters the height of the lid also increases.

On most 18-1/2" kettle grills (47cm), you can't prepare Beer Butt Chicken standing up on the grate. You have to switch to the lower charcoal grate. Furthermore, you have to consider that you do not have the entire surface of the grill grate in the kettle for indirect grilling. With this method, the meat does not lie directly over the charcoal. Therefore, when purchasing such an all-around device, a version at least a 22-1/2" (57cm) should be taken into consideration. This also makes it possible to grill for a larger number of people. It is also worth mentioning that the kettle grills from the Outdoor Chef Grill Company are equipped with a patented funnel system that offers effective protection from grease fire flames and bothersome smoke. Weber® kettle grills are alternatives. In the area of pedestal grills, models from the Barbecook® company are very interesting.

Electric Grill

This grilling device is especially suitable for smaller, spontaneous occasions. A large advantage is that in bad weather you can grill inside the house. It is the perfect device for all grill freaks who would like to be independent of the weather and season. With the water pan under the heating element, the dripping grease and the meat juice are caught. Thus, unpleasant odors are directly bound and after grilling the grease can be easily disposed of. Another advantage is that with proper handling no open flame forms and the fire danger is, therefore, relatively low. For larger barbecues, multiple electric grills must be used because the grilling surface is mostly smaller than fueled grills. Additionally, a standard table grill is not suitable for cooking larger cuts.

Smoker Grills

The large ovens — the so-called BBQ smokers — have a special role in the barbecue scene. In these seemingly archaic devices, a wood fire is kindled in the side firebox. Through an opening, the warm, smoky air of this fire flows into the closed cooking chamber in which the meat or other ingredients are heated on a grate. A flue at the other end of the cooking chamber draws the heat and smoke upward and ensures that a suction forms.

The heat in the BBQ smoker is controlled by various measures: the wood or charcoal (if it should taste less smoky) selection already decides how hot the fire will burn. A large fire naturally produces more heat than a small one. The ventilation flaps on the firebox and on the flue can regulate how much heat flows into the cooking chamber. The same applies to the intensity of the smoke that plays a decisive role in the smoker — as the name already implies.

To obtain the typical smoky flavor while barbecuing, you should preferably use aromatic woods. Fruit woods, such as wild cherries for example, are especially mild and appetizing. In contrast, walnut wood is stronger, which is recommended for meat like beef, bison, venison, or ostrich. Beech and oak are also very well suited for barbecuing, but do not use a resinous wood.

Advantages:

■ The meat does not need to be monitored or turned because it is evenly cooked all around at approximately 200–250°F (100-120°C).

■ The physical separation of the firebox and cooking chamber prevents grease or meat juice from dripping into the heat source.

■ This type of barbecuing takes little work and tastes excellent. Especially large pieces of meat are very well prepared in this manner, which, on the other hand, is only seldomly successful on a classic grill because the meat already becomes too dry on the outside while it is still raw inside.

Disadvantages:

■ You must allow for at least four hours of cooking time.

3. Suitable Fuels for Grilling and Smoking

Charcoal

Charcoal is not just charcoal. The same goes for both the wood used and the carbonization process during which the initial raw material wood is converted into combustible charcoal.

Good charcoal is always produced from unmixed wood, such as, for example, pure beech wood. If the manufacturer does not indicate the type of wood used, you can assume that wood residues from different types were mixed. In the worst case, waste wood would be used and that can possibly contain unhealthy residues.

Although the price is naturally never a guarantee, you can assume that expensive charcoal is normally also good charcoal.

Briquettes _____

For briquettes, small pieces of charcoal and charcoal dust, with the help of vegetable starch, mostly wheat or potato starch, are pressed into charcoal briquettes. They burn longer and hotter than broken charcoal, but are somewhat more difficult to kindle.

Spreading Charcoal:

The charcoal should be distributed approximately 2" (5cm) high and on all sides 2" (5cm) wider than the surface that you cover on the grate with the grill food. Distribute evenly.

Tip!

Coconut shells have a super heating value!

For indirect grilling or smoking, you should use a well-dried wood, such as mesquite, wild cherry, walnut, or Jack Daniel's Wood Chips!

Calculating the Charcoal:

How much charcoal you need depends on the type and amount of grill food. If you want to grill a lot, the fire must be long and really hot. It is always better to apply somewhat more charcoal than you think you need. You should consider that it is easier reducing heat instead of increasing it.

4. The Right Temperature for Grilling

Hand Test

Because grilling meat — as opposed to fish for example — requires a higher temperature, here are a few pointers for testing the heat: hold your hand palm down approximately 4-3/4" (12cm) over the charcoal and count the seconds until you need to pull away:

– After 1 to 2 seconds = high heat
– After 3 to 4 seconds = medium to high heat
– After 5 to 6 seconds = medium heat
– After 7 to 8 seconds = low to medium heat
– After 9 to 10 seconds = low heat

Heat Regulation

The heat is reduced when you spread out the charcoal. To raise the heat, push the charcoal together and place new charcoal along the outside onto the fire.

5. Suitable Types of Wood for Grilling

"Fire made from straw has little value" — so it says in an Italian proverb. Wood, charcoal, and gas are valuable to heat kettles, smokers, and grills; however, because fire is not only fire, it is important to determine which fuel is suitable for your preferred grilling method.

People have known since primeval times that wood is a good fuel and have used it for themselves. In the modern kitchen, cooking is no longer done over a wood fire, but all the more at a barbecue — and with it the type of wood is decisive for the result. One thing in advance: wood should always be dry and healthy. Wood that is resinous or treated with chemicals, colors, or enamel should absolutely not be used. With a wood fire, the grill food should never lie directly over the flames — the fire is always kindled next to the grill food, so that the heat indirectly has an effect on the meat or vegetables.

Mesquite and Hickory

Throughout the United States, primarily mesquite and hickory are used for barbecuing. Both are types of walnut that are offered in supermarkets already chopped and dried.

Birch, Beech, and Oak

Wood from beech, birch, and oak is very well suited for barbecuing, even though the woods are different in a couple of aspects. Beech and birch wood burn at somewhat lower temperatures than oak wood and give meat and fish dishes an especially fine smoky flavor. The precondition for this is certainly that it is very dry and stored well. Otherwise, it will smell like damp jute while burning and transfer this flavor to the dishes. While oak wood develops a clearly greater heat, it is largely neutral in taste. The precondition here also is that it must be very dry and free from fungal infestation or pests.

Walnut

For dark meat from beef, bison, venison, or ostrich, professional BBQers naturally recommend walnut. Walnut wood reaches its full degree of ripeness when the trees are cut down in late autumn, at which time the lengthwise-split logs must be stored in an airy location for approximately two years — only then is the wood cut up in appropriate pieces of approximately 11-3/4" length (30cm) for barbecues and split again if needed. For a professional only, walnut wood that has been stored for at least three years is considered. In contrast, others swear by fresh wood. Many use only walnut that is cut fresh weekly.

Wild Cherry

Especially exquisite, an insider's tip among barbecue professionals is the wild cherry wood from central Europe. Wild cherries, particularly from the forests around Lake Constance (in Germany), deliver excellent results. These untreated woods grow in natural surroundings and have a thin bark. Primarily white meat — like pork, veal, poultry, or fish — get a fine flavor from it.

6. The Correct Way to Light Charcoal

Day after day in the summer you see people in their gardens or public parks who endanger their health and the lives of their children. Everything flammable is gladly thrown into the grill and ignited. Unfortunately, you read in the newspaper every summer about thoughtless grillers or curious children who are admitted to the hospital with serious burns. We would like to present you with the most widespread methods, with their advantages and disadvantages, for lighting charcoal.

Alcohol/Gasoline/Lamp Oil

School Grade: F

If you should feel too healthy or sick of your life, then this starting method suits you. Otherwise we would strongly advise you: Hands off!

Liquid Grill Starters

School Grade: D

As long as there is a certificate of approval mark on the packaging, you can use liquid starters without hesitation. Spread the charcoal flat in the heat source tray and evenly spray the charcoal before lighting. Unfortunately, most liquid starters stink horribly, and the guests and neighbors become concerned with unpleasant odors. After the fire has died out, you have to fan and blow to advance the heat.

Solid Grill Starters

School Grade: C

Solid grill starters are made from different materials, mostly in the shape of small cubes. With solid starters, charcoal or briquettes are piled up into multiple small pyramids. The cubes are then stuck in, kindled, and the live charcoal is spread. Also important here: certified-approved starters are food safe and do not cause damage when residues in the heat source burn away and the grill food lies above it. However, an absolute taboo is the cheap fire starters that stink terribly and leave behind a bitter taste on the meat.

In order to not have to wait forever, here the use of a hair dryer or another type of wind generation is recommended.

Electric Igniter

School Grade: C

Electric igniters are somewhat expensive, $15–$40, and function like a large immersion heater. However, note that the electricity meter turns twice as fast.

Hot Air Gun or Large Bunsen Burner

School Grade: B

With this the heat source, a charcoal grill is quickly kindled. It is well-known that hot air guns are very universal devices. Also, at a barbecue in a garden, they can provide valuable services because you don't need any matches — only hot air. At an air temperature of approximately 1,100°F (600°C) and more, the charcoal ignites all on its own. At the same time the air flow serves as a convenient substitute for bellows. For lighting, it is sufficient to blow the hot air (highest temperature setting, lowest air flow) into the charcoal for only a few minutes. Already after a few seconds, the fine charcoal dust ignites. The strong air draft quickly drives the flames through the charcoal so that in no time a wonderful heat source for grilling develops — you only need a socket. Almost the same goes for the Bunsen burner. However, it is very immovable due to the large gas cylinder, but you will create a sensation with it before the barbecue begins.

Charcoal Starter

School Grade: A

The best and unfortunately still too unknown aid for grilling is a charcoal starter, which quickly and easily lights the charcoal in a container. Place a fire starter cube or also crumpled-up newspaper on a heat-resistant base or on the grill's charcoal grate and ignite it with a long-handled lighter. Fill the charcoal starter with the necessary amount of charcoal. Place the filled charcoal starter over the burning cubes. After fifteen to twenty minutes, the charcoal is covered with a white-gray layer of ash and is ready for the grill. Using the charcoal starter handles, place the hot charcoal onto the charcoal grate and distribute the charcoal evenly according to the direct or indirect grilling method.

A charcoal starter functions as follows: Warm air rises and escapes upward. From this, a sub-pressure develops that is balanced from the flow of air. This fresh air contains more oxygen that continues to fan the fire. From this, the temperature in the charcoal starter rises, and more air is heated and rises. Physics can be so beautiful!

Tip!

Charcoal starters have different qualities and capacities. Do not buy a charcoal starter that is too small and, above all, when purchasing put emphasis on solid workmanship and material quality. In the charcoal starter, temperatures are easily several hundred degrees, which makes heavy demands on the material. It is the old truism: "If you buy cheap, you buy twice." A proper charcoal starter is almost an investment for life and not just for one season. The Weber charcoal starters have proven themselves to be the best.

7. Grilling Accessories

The grilling accessory market is constantly growing and is a paradise for grillers of the world. What the shoe stores are to the girls is what the barbecue shops are to the boys.

Basic Grilling Equipment

Charcoal Shovel

After the barbecue, many ashes and charcoal that are still burning accumulate. A metal shovel provides an especially good service here. It offers much transport capacity and cannot melt. It is also suitable for removing the heat source from a campfire.

Trowel

Small amounts of charcoal and ash can be transported with a commercially-available trowel.

Grill and Charcoal Starters

For more information on these, see section 6.

Matches, Lighter

You need grill lighters to start a fire. Matches are to be used only on a limited basis if there is strong wind. There are stick lighters with an adjustable flame. Mostly all have an electric igniter and are made of metal — thus the wind has no chance.

For Around the Grill

Side Table

A storage surface next to the grill that is not too small is essential because everything that is needed for grilling must stand ready here: marinades, hand towel, grill food, drinks for the grill boss, and a storage area for tongs and other utensils. Simple camping tables that quickly fold up are also suitable.

Grill Box

Store your most important utensils in a metal or hard plastic box or cabinet that is near the grill. Here you will find everything you need for starting fires and grilling sheltered from the rain: lighter, starter, and much more. Having a grill box also means you don't always have to laboriously search and can carry the box into the basement and store there as needed.

Tongs

Charcoal Tongs

To disperse the charcoal or specifically arrange the briquettes, you will need tongs that are as long as possible. Otherwise the heat on the grill will in no time burn at least the little hairs on your hands!

Grill Tongs

It is unappetizing to use the tongs soiled with charcoal dust for the food. Therefore, you should have additional tongs available to handle food.

Tip!

Tongs are better suited for turning instead of a fork because you have a good grip on the meat and your hand is farther away from the heat source. Additionally, the meat is not perforated here, which, with sensitive pieces, such as steaks, allows the meat juice to escape.

Other Accessories

Drip Pan

Everyone who buys a kettle grill receives a few aluminum pans included from the manufacturer for indirect grilling. Unfortunately, these are used up rather quickly because the cleaning is more than difficult, and already after a few hours of use you have to dispose of them. In every large supermarket, there is a culinary department in which different baking pans are sold. A worthwhile purchase is a stainless steel pan for under $15 that is easy to clean and much larger than the aluminum pan.

Caution with Teflon-coated pans: the alloy dissolves quickly at high temperatures.

Cleaning Brush/Scouring Pad

After grilling, the grate should always be cleaned. This is done quickly and with little effort with a steel brush or a steel wool pad.

Grill Thermometer

If you want to measure the inside temperature of your kettle grill while indirectly grilling, you are either lucky and your model already has a built-in thermometer. Or you use an oven thermometer that is placed into a ventilation opening in the grill. These bimetallic thermometers can be purchased starting at $15). However, make sure that the temperature scale reaches at least 575°F (300°C).

Fish Basket

With the fish basket, you can easily turn entire fish or fish fillets on the grill without them falling apart.

Skewers

Made of Wood:
They are cheap in large numbers for one-time use (even in bamboo). However, you should soak the skewers before use to prevent them from charring.

Made of Metal:
Make sure that the skewers are flattened so that the food doesn't slide off when turning. They should also not be too long because then you may potentially be unable to close the lid of your grill or have problems positioning on the grate.

Tip!

Leave the grate on the grill until the ashes have cooled down. The remaining heat source pyrolizes the build-up on the grate, and it can be removed easily.

Poultry Shears

To carve up chicken or larger, indirectly grilled poultry, poultry shears are indispensable. It makes the cutting of poultry child's play.

Silicone Brush

This brush is hygienic and durable. It optimally spreads grease, oil, and marinade evenly. The special synthetic bristles are heat-resistant and easy to clean. Silicone brushes stand temperatures up to 575°F (300°C) and can easily be cleaned in the dishwasher. Plus, they are not only suitable for grilling, but are also indispensable aids in the kitchen. Their greatest advantage: they don't lose hairs!

Tip!

A seasoning alternative is a rosemary brush: tie several rosemary sprigs onto a little stick with florist wire and you can apply marinade or oil with it.

Aluminum Foil

Especially with indirectly grilled poultry, it is possible that many parts — like the wings or breast — become dark too quickly. During the cooking process, you can make "heat shields" out of aluminum foil for the affected sections and the chicken or duck will be evenly cooked. Aluminum foil is also used to cover steaks and larger pieces of meat when resting so that they do not lose too much temperature and become nicely juicy.

Digital Meat Thermometer with Temperature Probe

A meat thermometer should have the following qualities:

1. Magnetic Base: It can be attached on almost all metal objects except the grill itself: danger of overheating!

2. Timer Function: Countdown function to a predetermined core temperature or alarm function at a set time period.

3. A Probe with a Long Cable: The grill food is always monitored and the display is outside of the grill or smoker. Expensive models offer a radio with the measuring probe. During your daily cooking you will be really delighted with it and you'll never want to do without it!

Spices/Mill

Freshly ground spices have an intense flavor. You should definitely choose them over the already-ground spices. Spice mills are inexpensive to get and can be filled with salt (refined salt), peppercorn, or chili peppers. A mortar also serves well.

Carving Board

A board that is not too small offers the opportunity to carve poultry, and there is also room for larger roasts. The grill food can then be carved near the grill. Wooden boards are inexpensive and offer sufficient stability and the required hygiene for poultry and meat.

Kitchen Knives

A large and solid chef's knife should be included in the basic kitchen equipment. You can cut up vegetables and meat with it and easily take care of the usual tasks.

Boning Knife

For precision work, such as removing bones and filleting, you need an especially sharp and small knife with which you can work more finely.

Meat Cleaver

To cut lamb or pork chops, you need a heavy cleaver. Otherwise, you would ruin your knives that you have grown to love!

Diamond Sharpening Stone

Pull the knife blade on the grinder twice on each side at a 20 degree angle and the knife is as sharp as it was the first day. Conventional sharpening steels by far do not offer the sharpening factor like this tool, which is coated with diamond dust. Alternative: Whetstone.

Metal Turner

To turn over hamburgers without damaging them, you need a sturdy tool without a plastic coating.

Cast Iron Grate

This essential gadget helps every grilling sports person to create a wonderful branding on the meat and cook the meat without burning it. Heat for a few minutes on the grill, oil lightly, and place the meat on top. After grilling let burn out, oil again, and the cast iron grate is ready for the next grilling. For kettle grills, patented cast iron grates are recommended.

Rib Rack

With two entire baby back ribs, the indirect grilling surface of commercially available devices is mostly used up. A rib rack remedies this. The ribs are placed vertically into the stainless steel device, and the number of ribs to be cooked is increased by a factor of at least 5.

Chicken Roaster

Poultry that is indirectly grilled "sitting up" needs a stable base. Of course, you can use beer cans or jars, but special stainless steel containers have proven themselves as a durable acquisition for life: a pipe stands vertically on top of a quadratic or round base. The liquid that is to evaporate is filled into the pipe and the chicken with the body cavity is placed on top. The secure stand and the easy cleaning afterwards is pleasing!

Rotisserie with Basket

Many grill manufacturers offer rotisseries that are operated and turned by batteries, but there are also solutions for larger grill food: a resourceful tinkerer who uses truck windshield wiper motors in a manner that wasn't intended for purchasing electric motors with high torque from online auction houses.

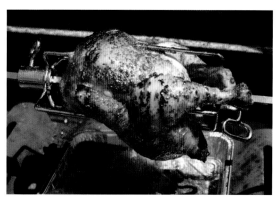

Vacuum Device

Naturally, you sometimes prepare somewhat more and want to freeze it, so then you have to immediately put purchased meat into a freezer bag and extract the oxygen with a vacuum device. Thus, it lasts longer. Vacuum devices are available starting at $25 dollars. For a bit more, you can purchase semi-professional machines that make freezing and vacuuming fun.

Butcher's String

This is a somewhat thicker, food-safe string that can be used to wrap around rolled roast or to bard venison with bacon. In supermarkets, this product is rarely encountered, but for a little bit of money the string is found on online auction houses and by mail. Certainly a butcher you trust will sell you a few feet (meters).

Gloves

Heat-resistant gloves are almost an obligatory for ambitious grillers. For larger grill operations, you have to stand at the grill for a long time and handle the heat source often. Charcoal starters and steel grills commonly cause burns on the inside and outside surfaces of the hands. Gloves protect to a certain degree, and you can move charcoal by hand should it be necessary. Additionally, these gloves protect your hands from the radiant heat at the grill.

Sturdy Shoes

Make sure that you do not grill barefoot or in sandals. When turning over the charcoal, sparks and cinders fly around that can cause unpleasant burns. Even more dangerous is hot grease, sauce, or the liquid from the drip pan. Certainly you have a pair of old shoes in the basement that can get somewhat dirty and stand burn holes.

Napkins

With many dishes, like spare ribs, you should have no reservations about eating with your hands. However, you should also offer your guests the opportunity to clean their hands. So that your house is not marked by greasy fingerprints of your family members or guests, it is best to provide a sufficient amount of napkins. I'm sure they would also appreciate water bowls with lemon slices in which they can clean their hands.

8. Shopping List for Barbecuing and Grilling

Nothing is worse and more embarrassing than the following situation: You have invited a lot of friends to a cozy BBQ. It is Sunday, you start up the grill, and delight in the ritual. However, this is just when you, the boss of the grill, realize that something is missing. Unfortunately, the first guests arrive right at that moment ... this doesn't have to be. The ultimate shopping and check list helps everyone with planning a successful barbecue.

Drinks	Around the Grill	What May Also be Present
Beer	Charcoal	Candles
Soft drinks	Briquettes	Tea lights
Mineral water	Matches, lighter	Torches
Sparkling wine, wine	Grilling gloves	Music system
Spirits	Grill tongs	Umbrella
Punch	Charcoal starter	Umbrella stand
Cocktails	Meat thermometer	Beer tables and benches
Champagne	Grill thermometer	CDs
Liquor	Cleaning brushes	Dishes
Aperitifs	Wood chips for smoking	Napkins
Instant cooler	Wood for grilling	Paper towels
Coffee, espresso, tea	Silicone brush	Sharp steak knife
Iced tea	Hand towels	Garden table
	Starters	Toys for children
	Fish basket	Streamers
	Grill apron	A bucket of sand
	Side table	Ointment for burns
	Hot stone	Aspirin
	Cast iron grate	Digital camera

Delicious Grill Food	Tasty Companions	For the Marinades
Poultry	Salad	Oil
Sausages	Dips, sauces	Soy sauce
Fish	Ketchup, mustard	Teriyaki sauce
Potatoes	Bread, baguettes	Worcestershire sauce
Vegetables	Mayonnaise	Paprika
Fruit	Flat bread	Honey
Veal	Spread	Red wine vinegar
Beef	Cream cheese	Pepper
Pork	Cheese	Ketchup
Venison	Couscous	
Onions	Tacos	
	Marshmallows	

9. Important Considerations for Buying Meat ___

The Quality of the Grill Meat ___

To be able to produce premium meat, in addition to the animal feed, livestock farming methods that are appropriate for each species is important. For the keeping of livestock, there are strict regulations to ensure quality. Of course, quality has its price. The farmer must raise the animals, feed and look after them for one to two years, and then he or she still needs state aid for the achieved sales revenue.

Local butchers work with high material and personnel use according to old tradition. For this, you also get choice quality, security, and freshness. Especially from a butcher you trust, you should be able to learn where the animals came from. If he or she doesn't want to give you the information, it is better if you change stores. Because imagine: a master butcher lies to his or her customers in his or her own establishment. For him or her and his or her staff and their families, this is economic suicide.

Selecting the Right Meat for the Right Grilling Method

Pork

Pork is a favorite meat — and rightly so. Among its advantages are the savory flavor, the versatile usability, the simple preparation, and the relatively inexpensive price. Premium pork has a strong pink color and a compact consistency. So that the flavor stands out, the lean meat should show a light marbling. Bacon should be as marbled and meaty as possible.

Pork is especially suitable for beginning grillers because here you can't do much wrong — grilled pork almost always becomes nicely tender. The reason: Pork is very poor in connective tissue, so you can grill practically all parts of a pig and the pieces seldom, if ever, become tough.

Suitable for Pork:

Direct grilling:
Stomach, chop, fillet (barded), neck steaks

Indirect grilling:
Rolled roast, spit roast, knuckle, spare ribs

IMPORTANT:
You should never eat pork rare or medium!

How to Grill a Suckling Pig

Shopping List

1   suckling pig
(For 18 people: 45 lbs. living (20kg), 35 lbs. grill ready (15kg); grilling time: approximately 6 hours)

25 lbs.   charcoal (10kg)
50-90 lbs.   wood briquettes (20-40kg)

Seasonings

1-3/4 cups   salt (500g)
1/2 cup   coarse pepper (50g)
5   garlic cloves
                some caraway seed
                paprika, hot
4 cups   sunflower oil (1 liter)

Preparation

Precise planning of a party and timing is important during preparation for grilling: the day prior, you should thoroughly season the pig inside and out so that the salt can be really absorbed. Alternately, you can have the suckling pig professionally seasoned and the skin scored at the butcher's shop — this also has the advantage that the pig is stored cool shortly before grilling.

■ Crush the garlic, mix with pepper, paprika, and oil, and rub the inside of the ribs. (If caraway seed is desired, grind it and mix with the garlic-oil paste.) Combine the paprika-pepper and oil and rub the outside of the pig with it. Carefully score the skin with a good knife in a diamond pattern.

■ Secure the suckling pig on a spit. In the process, tie the front feet closely to the cheeks (preferably with a thick wire). Tighten the hind legs backward, sew up the stomach with wire, wrap the pig in a cloth, and store in a cool place for the upcoming day.

■ Light half a bag of charcoal until a nice heat source develops. Assemble the spit on the supports and slowly begin grilling with a good distance from the heat source. Evenly brush the skin on the outside with oil.

■ It is helpful (and saves charcoal) to spread the charcoal in the shape of a dog bone. For the first hour of grilling, have a very thin strip of charcoal in the center; later have two larger piles at the front and back. The heat automatically moves toward the center! Occasionally, add new charcoal to the edge and later spread these evenly.

■ During grilling, the pig begins to "sweat." For this reason, you should oil the skin at regular intervals (approximately every half-hour). After the first grilling hour, you can move the heat source closer to the pig — later gradually adjust to achieve a greater effectiveness of the charcoal. Depending on the size of the suckling pig, it takes longer until everything is finished. Keep measuring the temperature with a meat thermometer. At the end, brush with salt water. The finished suckling pig has a core temperature of at least 160°F (70°C) all over — a temperature of 160–175°F (70-80°C) is ideal.

Tip!

If heat blisters form, poke them with a point. If the skin loosens from the meat or splits open, secure it with small metal skewers.

Beef

The differences in quality are as diverse as the cuts of beef. They are largely dependent on from which sections the meat comes. The sex (bull, cow) and age of the animal also play an essential role. The older the animal, the more interconnected the connective tissue is, which means the firmer the meat is. The breed from which the beef comes is also important, as well as how it is fed and kept. Mostly beef from young bulls is offered for sale.

Beef is very well suited for grilling. It is rich in protein and minerals. Also, the fat content is less than pork.

So that the beef becomes nicely tender on the grill, you should only use pieces that do not have much connective tissue. These are pieces from the haunch, loin, and fillet. Meat with too much connective tissue becomes tough during direct grilling and tastes like rubber. In addition, beef steaks should show a slight, light white marbling of fat. This ensures that the pieces will become nicely tender.

Suitable for Beef:

Direct grilling:
Steaks like chateaubriand (double fillet steak), entrecote (from the center of the roast beef), porterhouse, t-bone, rib eye

Indirect grilling:
Center cut brisket, whole roast beef

Steaks

There is a great variety of steaks to choose from here in the U.S. They are cut in different variations from sirloin.

Probably the best beef steaks are the t-bone, porterhouse, and rib-eye steaks. The further inward you go in the sirloin, the more tender and higher quality the meat.

The porterhouse steak has the biggest fillet portion and is actually a combination of two pieces of meat: roast beef and fillet. The name appeared in New York in 1841. Restaurants that served "porter's ale," a dark strong beer for port workers, were called "porterhouses." One of these restaurants served exactly this steak as a specialty; thus, the name went around the world. It has a weight of 1 to 1-3/4 pounds (500-800g) and a thickness of 1-1/2" to 2-1/2" (4-7cm).

Next to the porterhouse steaks are the t-bone steaks. Since the fillet has a pointed shape, the fillet portion decreases with additional pieces. The t-bone steak received its name from the t-shaped bone that separates the fillet from the roast beef.

Rib-eye steaks are cut from the prime rib. It is named for the clearly visible fat core, the "eye." This marbled meat is especially tender and tasty and is perceived by many to be one of the best steaks. Uncut, the piece of beef is called "rib roast," and this festive roast is the best that you can get from beef.

Preparation

Too much seasoning can destroy the steak's own excellent taste. Therefore, the steaks should be prepared in a traditional way. Season with pepper, grill on a hot grate, on both sides, with high heat, let rest in aluminum foil for at least five minutes, and then sprinkle with sea salt.

Especially popular in the U.S. are spare ribs. They are twice as large as those from pork and also offer a lot more meat content. They are well suited for indirect grilling, but can also be prepared in a low-temperature process.

Lamb

What is special about lamb meat is that is comes from very young animals. Therefore, it is not only very lean and fine-fibered, but it also possesses a highly subtle, delicately spicy flavor. Premium young lamb is recognized by its appetizing red color. A slight marbling furthers the fine flavor and causes it to remain juicy during preparation.

Suitable for Lamb:

Direct grilling:
Chops, fillet

Indirect grilling:
Leg, saddle

Poultry

Chicken and turkey taste the best when you grill individual pieces with the skin because the fat in the skin makes the meat nicely tender and it doesn't dry out so fast. However, in the supermarket, pieces of poultry are only rarely offered with the skin. Therefore, choose whole poultry and cut up the pieces yourself. If it is too complex for you, purchase the already cut-up pieces without the skin. However, to make sure the meat does not burn and remains tender, you should first sear the poultry breast and cutlet on the hottest spot of the grill (in the center) for two minutes on both sides. This way the pores will close, preventing the juice from escaping outward and the meat becomes tender. Afterwards, simply move the pieces to the outer edge of the grill that is not as hot and continue to cook.

Important!

Due to the risk of salmonella, poultry must never be eaten rare or medium. Only when the meat is well done are all pathogens really killed.

Suitable for Chicken:

Direct grilling:
Wings, breast fillet

Indirect grilling:
As a whole (Beer Butt Chicken), leg

Suitable for Turkey:

Direct grilling:
Cutlet

Indirect grilling:
Leg or as a whole

How to Choose the Right Piece of Meat

Many types of meat cannot be grilled immediately after being slaughtered. After being slaughtered, beef should hang for approximately three weeks for briefly cooked cuts. Lactic acid forms in the muscle fibers that changes the protein of the meat and with this develops its structure. The meat becomes tender, better to digest, and gets its typical flavor. Pork needs only to hang for forty-eight hours. Veal comes from young cattle that are at most four months old. It should hang for only two to three days.

Remember: High quality meat may be lightly streaked with fat; for grilling it should be slightly marbled. This refers to a subtle streaks of fat in the muscle that melts during grilling and ensures that the meat remains juicy and tasty. A subtle fat edge also protects the meat from drying out.

Tips for Choosing the Right Piece of Meat

■ The Meat Looks Appetizing: Pay attention to how the meat is offered for sale. The store should make a hygienic and clean impression. The cut surfaces should be dry. If the meat is flabby, has a pale color, and already a lot of meat juice has escaped, or it is very dark and sticky, this is indicative of poor quality.

■ The Meat Should Be Correctly Proportioned: Make sure that your grill pieces are always cut against the grain. This results in tender, short meat grains. The thickness of the slices should be at least as thick as a finger for grilling. Classic steaks can be even thicker. If the meat is cut too thin, it will quickly dry out during grilling.

Freshness of the Meat and Best Way of Preserving Meat

Freshly purchased meat should always immediately be placed in the refrigerator, especially in the summer. It is best to bring a cooler bag with you when making a purchase. In the refrigerator, you can keep poultry for a maximum of two to three days, pork a maximum of three days, and beef no longer than four to five days. Meat has the best flavor and aroma when you enjoy it on the same day.

In general, cut up meat spoils more quickly than whole meat (for this reason use minced meat as soon as possible). Vacuum-packed meat can be kept correspondingly longer (the "best-by date" must be indicated on the label). The use of a vacuum sealer is also recommended, as it extends the preservability by several days.

How to Correctly Freeze Grill Meat

Place the purchased meat immediately in a freezer bag and remove the air beforehand with a vacuum-sealing device. This will help keep it longer; there is no frost burn and it makes thawing out the grill food easier. At approximately 0°F (-18°C), all micro-biological processes have ceased and can no longer harm the meat, though most vitamins and minerals will survive. However, you should not keep the meat longer than six to twelve months in the freezer.

What is Important for Frozen Poultry

- Thaw out overnight in the refrigerator

- Completely thaw out the meat so that lit will cook evenly

- Drain the liquid from thawing — risk of salmonella!

- Remove the insides

- Rinse off thoroughly inside and out

- Blot dry the skin with paper towels

- Prepare as quickly as possible — risk of salmonella!

- Never re-freeze thawed meat

When Is the Meat Done?

In the recipe instructions, the cooking times are mostly provided, but no two pieces of meat are alike, so personal experience is required in order to bring a tasty meat and grilled meal to the table. Determining the doneness of a piece of meat is most easily done by applying pressure with your finger. The more the meat gives way under the pressure, the less done it is. The needle test is more precise. You stick a thin meat needle through the surface to the approximate center of the piece. The color of the meat juice that comes out indicates the reached level of doneness. The doneness can also be determined by the internal temperatures of the pieces of meat.

The ideas of the doneness of meat are individually different — especially for steaks. Here we differentiate "blue," "rare," "medium," and "well done." Quick searing produces a steak gradation of "blue." You can also briefly carry the steak by the grill! If the inner meat temperature does not exceed 115°F (45°C) and the meat juice that comes out is still dark red, the steak is "rare." This doneness is reached after a minute-long searing and cooking for two minutes on each side until a thin, brown crust forms.

This cooking time applies to "normal" steaks of approximately 8 ounces (200g) weight; if they are very thick, the times must be extended correspondingly. If you cook a 8-ounce (200g) steak one to two minutes longer, the crust becomes thicker, the meat juice light red, and the center is still juicy: "medium" doneness. A steak is "well done" when the inner temperature has reached approximately 160°F (70°C).

Guidelines for cooking times for large roasts in the oven are approximately fifty minutes for each pound (500g) of beef and mutton, forty minutes for each pound (500g) of pork, and thirty minutes for each pound (500g) of veal.

Tip:

Cut the cooked meat only after five to ten minutes of resting; otherwise, too much of the roast juice escapes and the meat loses its juiciness.

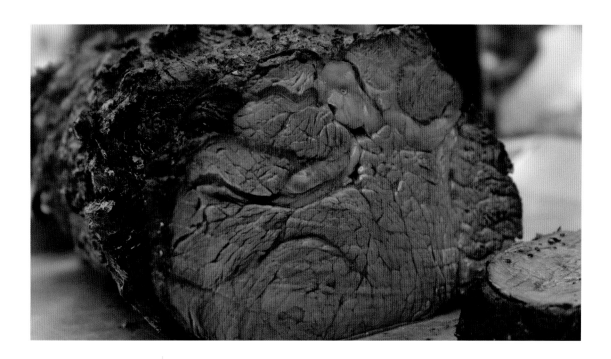

10. Grilled Fish — Healthy and Varied!

Fish is ideal for light cuisine. In addition to sausages and steaks, it has established itself as a staple in recent years. Whether skewered, stuffed, or folded — the trend is Mediterranean grilled fish specialties with refined, exceptional, and, at the same time, simple recipes. With a little skill and finesse, you can easily prepare a gourmet delicacy on the grill. There are a few points to note, and with the following tips, your grilling season will be full of success.

Herring, Gilthead Bream, and Co.

In principle, all types of fish are suitable for the grill; firm and high-fat are especially well-suited. Here is a variety of the selection available: herring, mackerel, sprat, red mullet, swordfish, trout, salmon, eel, rosefish, halibut, tuna, gilthead bream, and sea bass.

Likewise, delicious delicacies from the grill are squid, shrimp, and lobster. Fish is also available ready to cook for the grill at food retail markets. Refined with marinades or interesting mixed spices, they are prepared in minutes. Just the right thing if you, despite little time, do not want to go without delicious grill specialties.

Tips for Purchasing Fish

Look the fish in the eyes. They should be clear, round, and protruding. The gills of a fresh fish should have a red to pink color and, when opened, a few threads of slime. The individual gill lamellae should be clear and easy to recognize. The entire fish should have moist and shiny skin without tender spots, as well as tight scales. A mucous layer on the skin is also an indication of freshness. The cavity of a gutted fish should be properly cleaned. When purchasing, the fish fillet should be moist and shiny.

Pay attention to the odor of the fish.
Fresh fish hardly has any odor!

Perfect Storage

Ideally, fish should be purchased on the day of preparation. It is best stored in the refrigerator when it is previously taken out of packaging and placed into a neutral container. If you cover it additionally with foil and ice, you can leave it in the refrigerator for up to one day.

Frozen fish should be used before the expiration date. Optimally, it should be defrosted in the refrigerator and the water should be able to completely drain. You should keep the fish well chilled until shortly before grilling. This is best done when you store the fish in a pan on ice or in a cooler next to the grill.

Marinades – Herbs and Spices Provide an Extra Something

Before you actually grill, you can improve your fish with herbs and spices. Marinades provide an intense flavor and are prepared easily yourself.

For marinating, liquid marinades with an oil, vinegar, wine, or soy sauce base are best suited. There are no limits to the imagination here. Herbs and spices, such as parsley, dill, tarragon, oregano, garlic, etc., can additionally improve the marinade.

So that the flavors spread better over the fish, for white fish you deeply cut into the entire fish on both sides three to four times before marinating.

The fish should marinate at least two to three hours. It is recommended to turn the fish several times while marinating. So that no liquid drips into the heat source, you should blot it dry before grilling. If you have no time for marinating, lard the cuts with herbs or lemon/lime wedges. The cuts can be filled just as well with seasoned butter. In this case, the fish must be indirectly cooked so that the melting butter does not drip into the heat source.

Onto the Grate with Care

Fish and seafood are especially tender. For this reason, you need a little tact during preparation. The fish can easily burn or dry out. Therefore, the main rule is: the grate must hang over the heat source at a large distance so that the fish doesn't burn. It is also recommended — when possible — to only turn the grill food once.

Before grilling, you should oil the fish and grate well so that the skin doesn't stick to the grate. Seafood (such as shrimp) can best be lined up on a skewer so that they do not fall through the grate.

It can be helpful to use a special fish basket or grilling basket while grilling. Grill fish tongs are especially good for delicate fish. Fish that easily falls apart can also be wrapped in aluminum foil, but be sure to oil the aluminum foil well beforehand.

Grilling Time: Keep An Eye On the Clock

The grilling time depends on the thickness of the fish or fish fillet. As a general rule:

Approximately 3/8"-thick (1cm) pieces:
6 to 8 minutes

Approximately 3/4"-thick (2cm) pieces:
8 to 10 minutes

Entire fish (approximately 1" or 2.5cm thick):
10 minutes

Entire fish (approximately 1-1/2" or 4cm thick):
10 to 15 minutes

Entire fish (approximately 2" to 2-3/8" or 5-6cm thick):
15 to 20 minutes

Large shrimp with grilling tray:
5 to 6 minutes

Large shrimp without grilling tray:
3 to 4 minutes

To check if the fish is done, stick a knife into it and carefully open the flesh. If the inside is white and no longer translucent, the fish can be served.

11. List of Core Temperatures for Grill Meat

Pork

Food	Doneness	Core Temperature
Haunch/leg	well done	170°F (75°C)
Haunch/leg	light pink	150-155°F (65-68°C)
Pork loin	slightly light pink	150-170°F (65-75°C)
Pork neck	well done	160-170°F (70-75°C)
Pork shoulder	well done	170°F (75°C)
Pork belly, stuffed	well done	160-170°F (70-75°C)
Pork belly	well done	175-185°F (80-85°C)
Rear pork knuckle, roasted	well done	175-185°F (80-85°C)
Pickled knuckle of pork	well done	175-185°F (80-85°C)
Boiled ham	very juicy	150-155°F (64-68°C)
Rear knuckle, pickled	well done	170-185°F (75-80°C)
Ribs	well done	150°F (65°C)
Pork tongue	well done	185-195°F (85-90°C)
Kassler cold cuts buffet	pink	130-140°F (55-60°C)
Kassler	well done	140-155°F (60-68°C)
Pig's head	well done	170-180°F (75-82°C)

Beef

Food	Doneness	Core Temperature
Fillet of beef/loin	rare to pink	100-130°F (38-55°C)
Fillet of beef/loin	medium	130-135°F (55-58°C)
Roast beef	medium	130-140°F (55-60°C)
Thick flank	well done	185-195°F (85-90°C)
Brisket	well done	195-205°F (90-95°C)
Joint of beef	well done	175-185°F (80-85°C)
Tafelspitz	well done	195°F (90°C)

Veal

Food	Doneness	Core Temperature
Saddle of veal	light pink	150-160°F (65-70°C)
Haunch, leg, topside, knuckle, fricandeau	well done	170°F (78°C)
Kidneys	well done	170-185°F (75-80°C)
Roast veal	well done	155-165°F (68-74°C)
Veal shoulder	well done	170-185°F (75-80°C)
Breast of veal (stuffed or without bones)	well done	170-175°F (75-78°C)

Mutton

Food	Doneness	Core Temperature
Saddle of mutton	light pink	160-170°F (70-75°C)
Saddle of mutton	well done	185°F (80°C)
Leg of mutton	light pink	170-175°F (75-78°C)
Leg of mutton	well done	180-185°F (82-85°C)

Lamb: When well done, the core temperature amounts to between 175-185°F (79-85°C). The color in the center of the meat is gray, slightly pale red. The meat juice is clear.

Venison & Poultry

Food	Doneness	Core Temperature
Roast wild boar	well done	170-175°F (75-78°C)
Saddle of venison	well done	120-135°F (50-56°C)
Roast venison	well done	170-185°F (75-80°C)
Chicken	well done	175-185°F (80-85°C)
Duck	well done	175-195°F (80-90°C)
Turkey hen	well done	175-195°F (80-90°C)
Goose	pink	170-185°F (75-80°C)
Goose	well done	195°F (90-92 °C)
Turkey cock	well done	175-185°F (80-85°C)

Fish

Food	Core Temperature
Salmon	140°F (60°C)
Pike	145°F (63°C)
Fish mousse	150°F (65°C)

Other Grilled Dishes

Food	Core Temperature
Pâté	160-165°F (72-74°C)
Meat loaf	170°F (70°C)
Tureens	140-170°F (60-70°C)
Galantines	150°F (65°C)
Ballotines	150°F (65°C)
Foie gras (goose liver pâté)	115°F (45°C)

12. Brining and Brine: It Can Be So Simple

What is Brining?

Some chickens or turkeys are tough like tar paper and dry like sawdust. Others, on the other hand, are juicy, spicy, and tender. Where do the differences come from? The answer is: brining.

The basic principle is very simple: a solution of salt, often sugar, and a liquid, normally water, is made, and the grill food is placed in it. The meat becomes saturated with the liquid, which it will retain during cooking. The turkey or chicken will put on some weight because it has absorbed the water. The salt and sugar are then soaked into the meat and gently season it.

The Best Brining Candidates

The leaner and less flavorful types of meat, such as chicken, turkey, or pork, are perfect for brining. Also, many types of seafood can be treated in the same manner, especially when exposed to methods of preparation that cause a high loss of liquid. Some examples are

Chicken: Whole and pieces

Seafood and Fish: Salmon fillet, shrimp

Pork: Fillet, chops, ham

Turkey Cock and Turkey Hen: Whole and pieces

Salmon fillet is mostly not brined before direct grilling because it has enough fat and flavor and will not dry out when it comes from the grill. However, it must still be nicely shiny inside. If the salmon is put on the grill as an entire fillet with indirect heat or immediately into the smoker, then brining provides the ideal option that the fish spends enough time on the grill, can absorb the smoky flavor, and does not become too dry.

Shrimp, which are often extremely lean, are another dish that should be brined. The brine makes the shrimp especially firmer.

In contrast, brining does not do anything for beef and lamb. These types of meat are eaten rare or medium and usually only cooked until a low core temperature is reached. Therefore, they do not lose much of their natural moisture like poultry or pork, which are generally prepared with higher core temperatures. Beef and lamb contain more fat, which makes them tasty and helps them stay juicy.

The Universal Formula for Brining

Brining is actually very easy.

■ In a container, mix cold water with salt and sugar and stir until the salt and sugar have dissolved.

■ Place the grill food into the brine, seal the container, and place it in the refrigerator. You can also use bags, but it is recommended to use these doubled so that you are safe from leaks in the refrigerator.

Basic Brine:

(1 quart per pound/2 liters per kilogram of meat)

1 quart (liter)	cold water
1 cup (250g)	salt
1 cup (250g)	sugar
1 hour per pound, but no more than 8 hours	

High Temperature Brine:

(1 quart per pound/2 liters per kilogram of meat)

1 quart (liter)	cold water
1/2 cup (125g)	salt
2 tbsp.	sugar
1 hours per pound, but no more than 8 hours	

Of course, you can use less salt (2 to 3 tablespoons) and leave the grill food in the brine for 24 to 48 hours. You just have to figure out this practical value over time according to your own taste.

What Can You Brine With?

Depending on the size of the grill food, you may need special containers, but, in day-to-day business, everyday objects always serve well:

In a Sealable Bag:
Chicken pieces, pork fillet and chops, shrimp

In a Cooler:
Whole turkey, entire ham, entire salmon fillet (with gel packs or cooling elements)

Tupperware® Container (or something similar):
Entire chickens

Gastronorm Containers:
The whole big whoppers

Tip!

If you own a vacuum sealer, you can speed up the brining process by placing a vacuum lid on the bowl and suck out the air inside.

Drying the Grill Food

Brining also has a negative effect on chicken and turkey. When the skin and meat absorb the moisture, it can affect the crisping of the skin during grilling. If the meat is air-dried in the refrigerator for a few hours, you can avoid the problem.

Recipes

Variations

Basically, you can brine with almost every liquid. All types of juices, like orange, pineapple, and apple, etc., are extremely suitable.

Salmon Brine

| 5 tbsp. | salt |
| 8 tbsp. | brown sugar to 1 quart of water |

Cola Brine

1 quart	cola
2 cups	orange juice
2 tbsp.	pepper, ground
4 tbsp.	salt
5	bay leaves
2 tbsp.	chili powder
2 tbsp.	paprika
2	onions
1 tbsp.	thyme
5 tbsp.	white wine vinegar

Juniper Brine

1 quart	water
1/2 cup (150g)	salt
3/4 cup (150g)	sugar
5	sage leaves
4	thyme sprigs
2	bay leaves
6	cloves
1 tsp.	juniper berries, crushed
1/2 tsp.	black pepper
2 tsp.	allspice berries, crushed

Buttermilk Brine

1 quart	buttermilk
1	onion
1	lime
3	scallions
3	garlic cloves
2 tbsp.	thyme
2 tbsp.	oregano
1 tsp.	cumin
1 sprig	rosemary
1 tbsp.	pepper
3 tbsp.	salt
2 tbsp.	soy sauce
3 tbsp.	cane sugar

Pork Brine

1/2 quart	water
3/4 cup (250g)	honey
1/4 cup (50g)	brown sugar
1	onion, diced
2 tsp.	pepper, ground
	some rosemary (very little)
1 pinch	salt
1 tsp.	mustard seed, ground
1	bay leaf

Herbs Brine

2 tbsp.	salt
2 tbsp.	sugar
3	bay leaves
3	garlic cloves
1 tsp.	thyme
1 tbsp.	oregano
1	large onion
1 tbsp.	honey
3 tbsp.	soy sauce
2 tbsp.	pepper, freshly ground
1	lemon, juice and flesh
2 cups	orange juice

Classic Brine for Pork
(such as knuckles)

1 cup	red onions, diced
6	garlic cloves, minced
1/2 cup	salt
1/2 cup	brown sugar
1 tsp.	thyme
1 tsp.	rosemary
3 tsp.	pepper
1 tsp.	paprika
1 tsp.	caraway seed
4	bay leaves

FBC –
Fruity Butt Chicken Brine ——————

juice	from 4 freshly pressed oranges
juice	from a lime
2 cups	apple juice
1 cup	beer
2	medium-sized onions
3	scallions
4	garlic cloves
10 slices	fresh ginger
2 tbsp.	fresh oregano
1 tbsp.	fresh thyme
2	chili peppers
2-1/2 tbsp.	salt
3 tbsp.	soy sauce
1 tbsp.	white pepper
1 tbsp.	coarse black pepper
1 tsp.	cinnamon
1 tbsp.	honey
3 tbsp.	sugar cane

Nifty Brine ——————

1 cup	orange juice
1 cup	lemon juice
1 tsp.	lemon zest
1/2 cup	pineapple juice
1 cup	salt
1 cup	sugar
1 cup	onions, diced
1/4 cup	coriander, chopped
1	bell pepper, diced
4	garlic cloves, minced
1 tsp.	chili powder
1 tsp.	oregano
1 tsp.	cumin
1 tsp.	nutmeg
8	allspice berries
10	black peppercorns
1	bay leaf

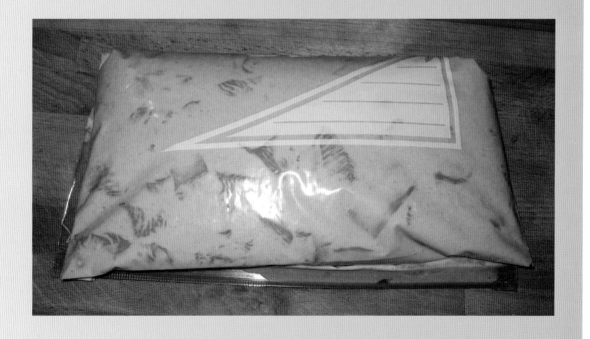

13. Spices Are the Icing On the Cake

Fresh Herbs and Spices for Grilling

Fresh herbs and aromatic plants like garlic and chili peppers give the grill dishes a wonderful, piquant flavor, so use them generously. Nowadays you can even get some of the herbs as potted plants for the balcony or windowsill in many produce shops and supermarkets. If you have enough space in your garden or on your windowsill, you can grow your herbs and spices yourself. Whatever is not used for cooking can be frozen with some water or ice cubes and be used later in sauces or soups. If no fresh herbs are available, you can use dried herbs — they also provide the dishes their special flavor, but they are not as aromatic as fresh herbs. Only buy dried spices in small amounts and use them as quickly as possible because over time they lose their flavor.

Spices Guide

Spice	Pork	Beef
Basil	■	■
Cayenne pepper	■	
Curry		
Dill		
Tarragon		■
Ginger		
Garlic	■	■
Herbs de Provence	■	
Lovage	■	■
Marjoram	■	■
Horseradish	■	■
Oregano	■	■
Paprika powder	■	
Parsley	■	■
Pepper, green	■	
Pepper, black		■
Rosemary	■	■
Sage	■	
Chives		■
Thyme	■	■

Lamb	Poultry	Fish
	■	
	■	
		■
	■	■
	■	■
■	■	■
■	■	■
■		
	■	
	■	■
■	■	■
■	■	■
■	■	
		■
■	■	

Fresh Herbs and Spices for Grilling:

Basil: Has bright green leaves and a very characteristic taste. It originally comes from India and is spread worldwide today. It is the main component of pesto, but is also used in salads. Its intense, spicy aroma gives dishes, especially tomato ones, a unique flavor. Whoever doesn't have room to grow it in the garden or on the balcony should have space for a little pot of basil in the kitchen.

Chervil: Delicate, feathery leaves and a mild flavor that is similar to parsley. It tastes somewhat like anise and goes well with fish. It is best used as subtle decoration because the leaves are delicate and will quickly wilt when heated.

Chili peppers: Available in different heat levels, from somewhat mild to blazing hot. If you measure them out properly, they give the dish a wonderful spice. Some fresh red or green chili peppers are extremely hot and should be used sparingly. Wash your hands immediately after contact with hot chili peppers and avoid contact with eyes or lips.

Chives: Belonging to the family of onions, chives are added to a dish just shortly before serving. They taste slightly hot, like the green of an onion. The purple flower heads can be eaten in the salad.

Coriander: Light green, pretty leaves and a fresh, slightly peppery flavor. Coriander wilts quickly. With some luck, you can store it wrapped in plastic wrap for two days in the refrigerator.

Fennel: A tuber with bright green, feathery leaves. It distinctly tastes like anise, and its leaves are similar to dill. You can enjoy the bulb as well as the stalk, raw or cooked. The bulb is mostly steamed as a vegetable or served raw in salads; the leaves are used as a seasoning.

Garlic: This necessary herb provides numerous dishes with their unique flavor; among these are meat, fish, and vegetables.

Lavender: Occasionally ground and sprinkled over chicken or pork. It also belongs to the mixed herbs of the herbs de provence (mixture of dried herbs), which are used for refining fish and chicken dishes.

Lemon balm: With a discreet, mild taste of lemon, it can be used in dishes with fish and chicken or in desserts.

Marigold: The blossoms are beautiful to look at and provide every salad with a special something.

Marjoram: A piquant spice with small, gray-green leaves and mauve or white blossoms. Thanks to its sweet, spicy flavor, it is often used in dishes with tomatoes, chicken, fish, or vegetables. It is the domesticated form of oregano.

Mint: A refreshingly versatile spice that appears in many forms on the market, mostly as peppermint. There is also mint in apple, lemon, pineapple, and ginger flavors.

Nasturtium: The leaves and blossoms of nasturtium are outwardly attractive and taste terrific in salads. The leaves have a typical peppery flavor.

Oregano: The wild form of marjoram. Like its cultivated cousin, it refines tomato, fish, and lamb dishes. In taste, oregano is stronger than marjoram.

Parsley: Comes in two forms: curly-leaf or flat-leaf. It is suited especially well for piquant appetizers and desserts or for soups and salads. The flat-leaf parsley tastes somewhat finer.

Arugula: A somewhat hot salad herb that in recent years has experienced considerable renaissance.

Rosemary: A wonderfully aromatic spice with a fresh and strong flavor, it is especially suitable for lamb or pork. You can also try it with fish or poultry, but be careful with the measurement.

Sage: A green plant with pink or mauve blossoms and typical velvety leaves; it is a very intense spice with a slightly bitter flavor and can be used for dishes with pork, veal, and poultry.

Tarragon: A spice with a characteristic flavor that goes very well with chicken or rabbit.

Thyme: A small, bushy shrub with gray-green leaves and tiny red or white blossoms. Thyme has a light, fresh aroma and a taste that is reminiscent of cloves. You can get it in different flavors, including lemon and apple.

14. Grilling around the world

"Grilling is a philosophy! Its deeper meaning lies within refining everything essential and burning everything irrelevant!"

Grilling – The Oldest Cooking Method in the World

An important step in the formation of human cultures and civilizations existed in the control of fire. It has been scientifically proven that humans have used it for more than 300,000 years, but presumably fire has been used for more than 790,000 years. Since this time, humans have prepared their food with the help of fire. Many studies have already focused on the history of grilling and they can be summarized as follows with few words: Man acquires food and stands at the fire to prepare it. With this, humans stand at the top of the social hierarchy!

Many "grilling historians" argue over the origin of the word "barbecue," with different theories existing. One states that the term originally stems from a word of a Haitian Indian tribe that describes how meat that is skewered on a green stick over a fire is cooked. Creoles could have brought the word with them to the American mainland, where the term "barbecue" was used for grilled meat. Until then, meat was also consumed unseasoned. The original meaning of barbecue presumably stems from the Mexican-Spanish word "barbacoa," which means "sacred fire pit." An additional explanation traces the origin of the term back to the French "Barbe à cul," which means "from the beard to the tail" and refers to the skewering and roasting of entire animals. Even the Romans already possessed skillfully worked grill grates in the fourth century AD.

In the United States, the mother country of grilling, it has always had a significant meaning. The poorer classes were initially enthusiastic about it; especially during the Great Depression and the economic upturn after the Second World War, the social gathering and food freshly prepared in this manner was treasured. At the beginning of the 1950s, the grilling phenomenon reached its way back to Europe, and for several years the grilling boom continued in Germany.

In English, the abbreviation BBQ is often used. In German-speaking countries, the matter is more complicated because in English, BBQ is often used as a synonym for the actual barbecue and also for grilling.

How Grilling is Done in Other Countries _____

Around the world trends have developed that are different and typical of specific regions. The variations are based on the follow facts:

1. The type of meat

2. The sauce that is served with it

3. The time at which the spices are added

4. The role of smoke during preparation

5. The equipment and fuel

6. The time spent

Generally, every source of protein is placed on the grill grate, whether it's beef, pork, poultry, or fish. Chopped up meat is also used, for example, in the form of minced meat or sausages. In addition, meat substitute products, like tofu, are grilled, as are a wide palette of vegetables.

Examples of Countries' Typical Characteristics

Australia and New Zealand

In Australia and New Zealand, barbecues are a popular pastime. There are even coin-operated grilling areas in city parks. The preferred grill food is marinated pieces of meat that are directly grilled or prepared over an open fire.

Grilling shrimp was practically still unknown in the United States until the 1980s, when a commercial with Australian actor Paul Hogan for the Australian tourism authority became popular: "Come on down here, and we'll throw another shrimp on the barbie for you!" (Of course, here they don't mean the "Barbie" doll from your daughter's room, but rather barbecue!) Especially popular at Christmas time in Australia are seafood BBQs. They are considerably better prepared with the warm temperatures than a large turkey in the oven.

Caribbean

The traditional preparation of jerk dishes is grilling on pimento wood over a pit in the ground in which fire smolders. In the process, the meat is rubbed with multiple seasonings.

Korea

The Koreans cannot do without bulgogi (grilled marinated beef).

Hong Kong

For the residents of Hong Kong, BBQs are an important component of excursions into nature. Normally beef, pork, or chicken wings are simply marinated with honey and grilled by hand over a heat source with long forks or skewers.

Mongolia

The typical dishes are a result of the original nomadic way of life: in the evening when the hunting party gathers around the campfire to eat, a shield, with the curved side placed upward, was put in the center over the open fire. At the same time the meat of the captured animals was prepared in extremely fine cuts with the sharp blades of the swords. When the shield on the fire had been heated enough, the meat was grilled on it. On a hot metal plate, the meat cooks in minutes. The pores close in the shortest amount of time, preserving the entire flavor of the meat. Today, not only meat is grilled, but vegetables and seafood are also very popular with a large selection of spices and sauces to refine the dishes.

South Africa

Probably the most typical South African food is always connected with a comfortable gathering in larger circles, known as "braai," an open-air barbecue event that goes back to the Boers, South African farmers with a Dutch heritage. Large amounts of beer and a vast number of "Boersewors" (Boer sausage — curled spirally), steaks, and chops (mostly from sheep) are consumed together with salads. The braai was originally an exclusively male event and was celebrated like an art: men comfortably stood around the grilling area with a bottle of beer while the women preferably were occupied with the preparation of the salads in the kitchen. Capetonians also like to grill fish, preferably snoek and yellowtail.

United States of America

The United States is considered the mother country of grilling. The regional differences are as correspondingly large.

Alabama

Spare ribs from pork and pork shoulder that are slowly cooked over hickory wood is typical here. Also, spicy-hot sauces with a tomato base are served.

California

The Arcata Bay Oyster Festival in mid-June offers a seemingly endless supply of oysters that are prepared by local chefs and also offered grilled.

Florida

Pork and seafood are prepared here with sauces made of butter and lime as a base.

Georgia

Generally barbecue in Georgia is based on pork, which is indirectly grilled on oak wood and hickory wood. The sauces contain ketchup, molasses, bourbon, and other ingredients.

Kentucky

In the Bluegrass State, barbecue has an especially long tradition. Here mutton is prepared in a smoker.

Mississippi

Many restaurants here specialize in serving only pulled pork. The upper portion of a pork shoulder is gently and very slowly indirectly grilled with smoke at a low temperature until the meat almost falls off of the bone and pulls apart very easily with a fork. The pieces of meat are then placed on a hamburger roll with a hot-sour sauce and topped with some coleslaw, which is likewise mixed with vinegar sauce.

Missouri

A simple and typical sauce here consists of ketchup, brown sugar, some mustard, and a shot of Worcestershire sauce. Also, chicken is gladly prepared in a smoker in the Show-Me State.

Tennessee

Memphis is well-known for ribs that are coated with a mild and sweet sauce before and after smoking. Spare ribs are also prepared with a dry rub. This is a dry marinade that is massaged into the meat before smoking. Chicken wings also enjoy much popularity here.

Texas

Here, the "holy trinity of barbecue" reigns: brisket, sausage, and pork ribs. This "holy trinity also symbolizes the status of barbecue for each Texan. At cook-offs, the meat is generally evaluated without sauce because it can too strongly interfere with the pure meat flavor.

"When I have eaten well, my soul is strong and unwavering, and the hardest blow of fate can change nothing about it."
Molière, French playwright and actor

"To me, life without veal stock, pork fat, sausage, organ meat, demi-glace, or even stinky cheese is a life not worth living."
Anthony Bourdain, celebrity chef and host of No Reservations

PART 2 The Recipes

Enough of the theory and history of barbecuing, here is a small selection of grilling recipes to get you started.

Good barbecuing!

Legend of Icons in the Recipe Section

 Charcoal grill

 Gas grill

 Dutch Oven

 Wood-fired oven

 Smoker

 Rotisserie

 Wok

Pork

Ingredients (serves 4)

Whole baby back ribs from the loin

Rub ————————————

1 tbsp.	salt
5 tbsp.	brown sugar
1 tsp.	chili powder
1 tsp.	thyme
1 tsp.	pepper

A container for mixing and a container for sprinkling

Sauce ————————————

1 cup	white wine
2 tbsp.	honey
2	garlic cloves
1 tbsp.	Tabasco, green
2 tbsp.	white wine vinegar
2 tbsp.	Worcestershire sauce

Preparation

■ From the specified ingredients, mix the rub and with it sprinkle the ribs and massage in well.

■ Wrap the ribs in two layers of aluminum foil and seal as a package. Place in the refrigerator overnight **(1)**.

■ The next day, mix a sauce from white wine, honey, garlic, Tabasco, white wine vinegar, and Worcestershire sauce and heat slightly so that the honey can dissolve. Carefully pour the sauce on the ribs in the aluminum foil and seal well again **(2)**.

■ Cook the whole thing in the oven, charcoal grill, gas grill, or smoker for 2-1/2 hours at 210-250°F (100-120°C). The ribs are done when you can easily twist the bones from the meat.

■ Cut open the foil over a pot, collect the liquid, and boil (approx. 10 minutes) until a syrupy consistency develops **(3)**.

■ Coat the spare ribs with it, place on the grill, and carefully brown. Note: The ribs become dark very quickly, therefore, grill at a moderate temperature and closely watch the meat! After approximately three hours, the ribs are done.

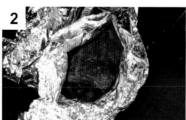

Florentine **Pork Roast**

Ingredients <small>(serves 4)</small>

Boneless pork loin (approximately 1-1/2 lbs. [750g])

2	garlic cloves
5	rosemary sprigs
	butcher's string
3 tbsp.	olive oil
2 lbs. (1kg)	carrots
1 lb. (500g)	zucchini
1 large can	tomatoes
1/2 glass	meat broth
1 glass	red wine
	tomato paste (a large shot glass)
	salt and pepper to taste

Preparation

■ In a small container, mix the finely chopped rosemary (1 twig), minced garlic (1 clove), salt, pepper, and olive oil.

■ Cut approximately four 3/8"-deep (1cm) pockets into the meat on each side with a sharp knife. Fill the pockets with the spice blend with the help of the knife point or a spoon. Keep the remaining spice blend (**1, 2**).

■ Tie four rosemary twigs to the roast with butcher's string.

■ Season well with salt and pepper.

■ Place the roast into the center of the oven.

■ Cut the zucchini into slices. Divide the onions into eight pieces and add potato pieces of approximately the same size as well as the remaining minced garlic on top.

■ Open a large can of tomatoes and cut the tomatoes one to two times; spread the remainder of the can contents over it.

■ Pour the remaining olive oil-spice blend over the bed of vegetables. Add the wine, meat broth, and tomato paste (**3**).

■ With plenty of top heat and medium bottom heat, cook for 70 minutes.

■ Cut the roast into slices that are not too thick and serve the tender meat on the bed of vegetables.

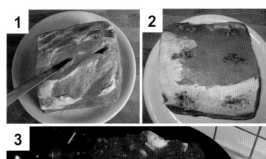

Ingredients (serves 4)

1	nice piece of pork belly, approximately 4 to 6 lbs. (2-3kg)
1 cup	butt rub or another strong rub
2 cups	orange juice
	salt
	water

Preparation

■ Cut into the belly rind with a sharp knife. With the rind facing down place in salt water for at least one hour.

■ Season the pork belly with the rub and marinate in the refrigerator for 24 hours.

■ Heat the smoker to 250°F (120°C) operating temperature and place the pork belly inside with the rind facing up for approximately 6 hours.

■ Turn the belly approximately every hour and spray with some orange juice.

■ After approximately 6 hours, place the belly on its rind again and move very closely to the firebox. Raise the temperature to 325-360°F (160-180°C) and grill for another 30 minutes.

Ingredients (serves 4)

4 strips	spare ribs from Ibericó pig
4 tbsp.	brown sugar
3 tbsp.	sesame
3 tbsp.	paprika powder
2 tbsp.	chili powder
2 tbsp.	garlic powder
	orange juice

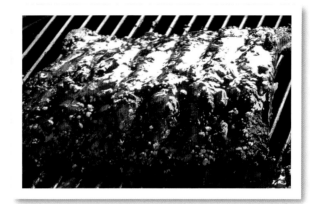

Preparation

■ Remove the silver membrane on the back side of the ribs.

■ Mix the sugar, sesame, paprika, garlic, and chili powder well and season the ribs on all sides. Wrap airtight and marinate for at least 12, but preferably 24, hours (**1**).

■ Heat the smoker to 250°F (120°C) and apply the ribs with the flesh side facing down for approximately 3-1/2 hours.

■ Turn the ribs for the first time after 2 hours and spray with orange juice. Repeat this process every 30 minutes.

■ The ribs are done when the bones can be pulled from the meat by hand. There is a total cooking time of approximately 6 to 7 hours because of the high fat content of the Ibericó ribs.

1

Ingredients (serves 4)

2 lbs. (1kg)	unpeeled potatoes, waxy
1/2 lb. (200g)	jerky or bacon
1-2	garlic cloves
10-1/2 oz. (300g)	leaf spinach
10-13	pork medallions
1-2 tsp.	mustard seed, ground
1 pinch	nutmeg
	paprika powder
	allspice
1 tsp.	vegetable broth
1/2 cup	white wine (Riesling)
1 container	cream
8	tomato slices (alternative: mushroom slices)
1/2 lb. (200g)	Parmesan, grated
3 tbsp.	rapeseed oil
1 tbsp.	butter

Preparation

■ Make a spice blend out of mustard seed, nutmeg, paprika powder, allspice, and vegetable broth.

■ Dice the jerky and render in a cast iron pan in a wood-fired oven (it also works on an electric plate).

■ Boil the unpeeled potatoes and then peel and cut into thin slices after they cool down. Season the leaf spinach with crushed garlic cloves and steam in a pan for approximately 10 minutes.

■ Cut the pork medallions from the loin and season on both sides with some salt and pepper, and then sear in a cast iron or iron pan in some rapeseed oil with butter.

■ Add 1/2 cup of good white wine to the medallions and sprinkle with the spice blend. Mix in the cream and boil for 2 to 4 minutes (1).

■ Prepare the small cast iron pan: place the potato slices on the base of the pan and then layer on the bacon sauce, spinach, and tomato slices. Finally, coarsely grate some fresh Parmesan over it (2).

■ Bake until crispy at approximately 390°F (200°C) for 15 minutes in the wood-fired oven over beech fire.

■ Instead of tomatoes, you can alternatively use fresh mushroom slices.

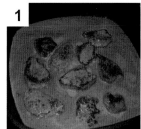

Pork Tenderloin **Roulades** with Bread Dumplings

Ingredients (serves 4)

2	pork tenderloins
	salt
	pepper
	paprika powder
	Tyrolean bacon

Bread dumpling dough

10	dry rolls
	flour
1 cup	milk
4-5	eggs (depending on size)
1	onion
	parsley
	pepper
	salt
	nutmeg
	bacon
	butter

Chanterelle cream sauce

1 tbsp.	capers
2 tbsp.	flour
2 tbsp.	butter
2 cups	meat broth
8 oz.	white wine
	cream
	chanterelle mushrooms
	salt
	pepper
1 small pinch	chili flakes
	nutmeg

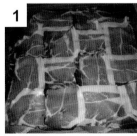 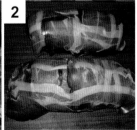

Preparation

■ Cut the pork tenderloin so that it can be rolled into a roulade. Season with pepper, salt, and paprika, but be careful with the salt because the bacon already provides salt. Coat with a portion of the bread dumpling mixture.

■ From the Tyrolean bacon, make a casing and roll the entire thing to form a roulade (**1, 2**).

■ Start the grill and grill the roulades indirectly for approximately 1 to 1-1/2 hours at 340°F (170°C). The roulades are done when they reach a core temperature of 165°F (75°C).

■ For the bread dumplings, cut the dry rolls into fine slices or cubes and place in a bowl. Briefly boil the milk and pour on top. Cover the bowl and let the rolls soak for approximately 20 to 30 minutes.

■ Finely dice the onion and bacon. Finely chop the parsley. Melt the butter in a coated pan. Briefly braise the onions, bacon, and parsley in it and add to the roll mixture. Add the eggs, flour, pepper, salt, and nutmeg and knead everything well. If the dough becomes too sticky, add some flour (it depends on the size of the egg).

■ With moistened hands, form bread dumplings that are the same size. In a large pot, bring enough salt water to a boil. Let the dumplings marinate in it for approximately 20 minutes at a medium temperature. As soon as they rise to the surface, they are done. Remove with a skimmer and drain well.

■ For the sauce, braise the capers and chanterelles in the butter, bind everything with flour, and let become light brown. Add the meat broth and wine and stir until smooth. When the liquid has somewhat boiled down, season once again. Finally, add a little bit of cream and reduce somewhat.

Ingredients (serves 4)

4	pork knuckles, weight per unit 2 lbs. (1kg)
4 quarts	water
1 tbsp.	sugar
10	bay leaves
1 tbsp.	juniper berries
1-1/2 cups (450g)	nitrate curing salt
	hot mustard
	black pepper

Preparation

■ Dissolve the nitrate curing salt in water and add the bay leaves and juniper berries. Choose a container size large enough for the knuckles to be completely immersed.

■ Wash the knuckles under running, cold water and place into the brine. Put the container in the refrigerator for 8 days **(1)**.

■ Fill a roasting pan with half a liter of water. Place a rack in it.

■ Coat the knuckles with mustard, sprinkle coarse black pepper on top, and place the knuckles on the rack. Close the roasting pan with the lid **(2)**.

■ Pre-heat the wood-fired oven to 480°F (250°C), insert the roasting pan, and cook for 90 minutes with decreasing heat to approximately 360°F (180°C). Relight as needed with a closed lid.

■ Remove the lid from the roasting pan and bake 45 more minutes at 320-360°F (160-180°C) **(3)**.

■ Dumplings and cabbage classically go well with this dish.

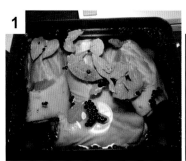

Ingredients (serves 6)

5 lbs. (2.5kg)	rolled pork roast of your choice (this recipe uses bread dumpling filling)
2 cups	beer (pilsner)
1-2 tbsp.	paprika
1 tbsp.	evaporated milk
1 tbsp.	oil

Preparation

■ For the mop sauce, mix the beer well with paprika, evaporated milk, and oil.

■ Pull the rolled roast onto the spit. Put the rotating motor at the back of the wood-fired oven. Heat the combustion compartment of the wood-fired oven with some beech wood and then add a charcoal starter full of charcoal briquettes. If necessary, fill the burning compartment with two additional firebricks to reduce the distance to the grill spit.

■ When the wood and charcoal are smoldering, place the spit in the rotating motor, turn on, and place the wooden handle of the spit in the additional support (baking compartment opening).

■ Let turn for approximately 1-1/2 hours, always monitoring the heat and meat, and occasionally basting the roast with the mop sauce.

Ingredients (serves 6)

6 portions	mini pork knuckles (small knuckles of pork without fat and rind)
	barbecue seasoning for vegetables
	knuckle seasoning with caraway flavor
1 cup (200g)	cooked cheese with caraway seed, full-fat
	pepper
	sea salt
3	pointed peppers
1	zucchini
8	shallots
10	cherry tomatoes
2 ribs	celery
10-1/2 oz. (300g)	mushrooms
3	mild chilies
1 bunch	scallions
1/2 bunch	basil
2 leaves	lovage
1	bay leaf
1 sprig	thyme
1 sprig	rosemary
1/2 bunch	parsley
12	medium-sized potatoes

Mop Sauce

2 cups	cider, sweet
1 shot	apple cider vinegar
	pepper
	salt

Preparation

■ Sprinkle the vegetables with sea salt, barbecue seasoning, and pepper.

■ Coarsely pluck the basil, lovage, bay leaf, thyme, and parsley, cut the scallions in rings, spread on top of the vegetables, and sprinkle everything with olive oil.

■ Wash the potatoes and, at an even distance of 3/4" (2cm), cut in crosswise up to approximately one half. Coat with melted butter and sprinkle with rosemary, sea salt, and coarsely ground pepper.

■ Rub the knuckles well with knuckle seasoning.

■ Heat the kettle grill to 290°F (200°C) and the smoker to 265°F (130°C).

■ Place the potatoes in a heat-resistant dish into the kettle and indirectly grill. Put the knuckles with the vegetables in the smoker, close the lid, and cook for approximately 2 hours. Regularly turn the knuckles.

■ Mix the mop sauce from the cider, some apple cider vinegar, pepper, and salt, and coat the knuckles with it approximately every half hour.

■ After 2 hours of cooking time, coat the potatoes with the cooked cheese and continue to cook until the cheese has melted and begins to brown.

Ingredients (serves 4)

8	ribs

Sauce

4 cups	orange juice
8 tbsp.	Worcestershire sauce
8 tbsp.	balsamic vinegar
12	garlic cloves, pureed
20 slices	ginger, grated
12 tbsp.	sugar beet syrup
4 tsp.	cinnamon
12 tbsp.	honey
8 tbsp.	Tabasco

Rub

2 tsp.	garlic, granulated
3 tbsp.	salt
10 tbsp.	brown cane sugar
2 tsp.	herbs and spice blend
2 tsp.	chili flakes
2 tsp.	thyme, dried
2 tsp.	pepper

Preparation

■ Make a rub from garlic, salt, brown cane sugar, herbs and spice blend, chili, thyme, and pepper.

■ Cut the ribs into pieces of 4 ribs each and rub with the rub.

■ For the sauce, put orange juice, Worcestershire sauce, and balsamic vinegar into a pot. Stir in the garlic, ginger, sugar beet syrup, cinnamon, honey, and Tabasco, and heat.

■ Place the ribs in pairs with the flesh side facing up on aluminum foil. Spread the warm sauce on the package and tightly seal the aluminum foil (**1**).

■ Cook the package in the smoker for 2 hours at 230-250°F (110-120°C).

■ Unwrap the ribs. Collect the sauce in a bowl, thicken to the desired consistency, and strain.

■ Finish the ribs in the smoker for one hour at 250°F (120°C) and in the process glaze 2 to 4 times with the sauce.

1

Ingredients (serves 4)

1	pork loin, approximately 21 oz. (600g)
1/2 lb. (200g)	smoked ham
1/2 lb. (200g)	bacon slices
	Magic Dust spice blend

Stuffing

1	tomato
1	onion
3	chilies, mild, from a jar
	some tomato paste
	gorgonzola cheese
	Emmentaler cheese, grated
3	garlic cloves
	brandy

Side dish

6-7	potatoes
2 to 2-1/2 cups	cream (500-600ml)
1	onion
	paprika, sweet
	salt
	pepper

Tip

A variation of loin stuffing consists of onions, garlic, finely diced, raw ham, and medium-aged gouda cheese. With this, the loin tastes savory and has a rustic touch.

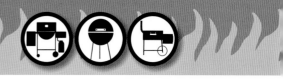

Preparation

■ Peel the onions, halve, and cut into fine strips and set aside half for the side dish. Finely dice the tomato, chilies, and garlic cloves.

■ Cook the onion strips until transparent and then add the tomato pieces, chilies, and garlic. Braise lightly, and season with some salt and pepper. Add some tomato paste, add brandy as desired, and set aside to cool.

■ Trim the loin; on the top side, cut into the center approximately 2/3 deep over the entire length. Turn over the loin; on the other side, cut twice lengthwise.

■ Unfold the loin and shape with the flat side of a meat tenderizer. The loin should be approximately as thick as a finger.

■ Season only one side with Magic Dust spice mix and, beginning at the edge to be rolled, cover 2/3 of the surface with the grated Emmentaler cheese.

■ On the front third of the loin, spread the cooled stuffing and place generously cut strips of gorgonzola at the edge in front **(1)**.

■ Tightly roll together the loin from the gorgonzola edge backward and place on the working surface to the rear.

■ Weave a ham-bacon net (see next page), place the loin on the lower beginning of the net, and carefully roll up. Fix the overlapping ends of the weave on the loin with toothpicks or roulade skewers **(2, 3)**.

■ For the side dish, wash the potatoes, peel, and cut into generous wedges. Because the potatoes need a considerably longer amount of time for indirect grilling than the loin, cook the potatoes for approximately 5 minutes.

■ Put the potato wedges into a stainless steel dish, pour approximately 2 to 2-1/2 cups of cream (500-600ml) on top, cover with the second half of the onion strips, and season with salt, pepper, and some paprika. For a fine flavor, add a few clumps of butter.

■ Indirectly grill the loin at approximately 320°F (160°C). Suitable for this is a kettle grill, a smoker, or an upright drum smoker — you can indirectly grill in each and achieve roughly the same result.

■ Place the stainless steel pan with the potato wedges in the kettle grill on the charcoal grate between the charcoal baskets, and place the loin on the grill grate over the stainless steel pan.

■ The loin should have reached a core temperature of 145°F (63°C) after approximately 1-1/2 hours. The loin can be coated twice — entirely according to preference — with a barbecue sauce of your choice during cooking time.

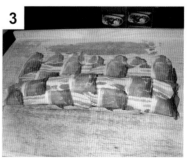

1. Place the bacon slices lengthwise in front of the loin, 6 rows from back to front. Slightly overlap the bacon slices.

2. In the center, from the top to bottom, apply a slice of smoked ham.

3. Now move the 1st, 3rd, and 5th bacon slices over the raw ham from left to right.

4. Then apply another slice of ham, put back the bacon slices that were moved, and fold the 2nd, 4th, and 6th bacon slices toward the right.

5. Apply ham again and weave with the bacon as described.

6. When the left half of the weave is finished, remove the slice of ham that was applied first, so that you can correspondingly fold back the bacon slices at this spot. Proceed with the right half exactly like the left half.

Peppered **Pork**

Ingredients (serves 4)

1 lb. (500g)	pork tenderloin
1/2 lb. (200g)	shallots or onions
2	bay leaves
2 cups (500ml)	meat broth
5 slices	bacon
4	cloves
1 tsp.	salt
2 oz. (50g)	green peppercorns, in a jar
1 tbsp.	paprika powder
1 cup	cream
1 cup	red wine
2 tbsp.	flour
2 tbsp.	vinegar

These quantity specifications fit exactly for one 10" Dutch Oven!

Preparation

■ Dice the tenderloin, add diced onions and bacon, bay leaves, cloves, and spices without browning.

■ Grind the soft green peppercorns in a mortar or with a fork and spread over the remaining ingredients **(1)**.

■ Pour the wine and meat broth on top, thoroughly mix in the flour and vinegar **(2)**.

■ After 70 minutes, the meat is as soft as butter and the sauce is thick **(3)**.

■ Serve with noodles or bread dumplings.

Pork Wellington

The Pork Wellington is a dish that was conceived by the Swiss chef Charles Senn on the occasion of the Zurich International Culinary Art Exhibition in 1930. It is pork tenderloin with a puree made of finely chopped mushrooms, possibly with pâté de foie gras (a smooth paste made from the liver of a specialty fattened goose), wrapped in puff pastry in a truffle sauce. It's named in honor of Arthur Wellesleys, the first duke of Wellington.

Ingredients (serves 4)

1/2 lb. (300g)	puff pastry
1-1/2 lbs. (750g)	pork tenderloin
1/2 tsp.	salt
1/2 tsp.	pepper
3 tbsp (4cl)	hot mustard
2	eggs

Sauce

1	shallot
1/2 lb. (200g)	bacon
1/3 lb. (150g)	mushrooms
1 tsp.	butter
1 tbsp.	mustard
1 tbsp.	tomato paste
1 cup	meat broth
2 tbsp.	Worcestershire sauce
1 tbsp.	cornstarch
1 tbsp.	paprika powder
1/2 tsp.	thyme
2 cups	cream
1 small can	tomatoes

Preparation

■ To simplify handling on the grill, it is best to cut the pork fillet into two equal pieces after cleaning.

■ Heat the grill and oil the grate. (Note: Oiling the grate is important because, since there is little fat on the meat, it would stick to the grate.) Brown the pork fillets on all sides at high heat **(1)**.

■ Season the meat well with salt and pepper and rub with the hot mustard. Don't worry, the mustard doesn't lose its hotness during cooking **(2)**.

■ Place the fillets in the puff pastry, put another layer of dough on top, and coat the edges with egg yolk. Join together and, using both hands, close the dough pocket. Brush both sides well with the remaining egg yolk **(3)**.

■ Place the dough packet on the grill over a drip pan filled with water and stick the roasting thermometer in one piece. Cook for approximately 60 minutes with indirect heat **(4)**.

■ In the meantime, prepare the sauce: brown the chopped bacon, shallots, and sliced, fresh mushrooms in butter. Add the meat broth, and then add the cream, tomato paste, diced tomatoes, and the spices. The mustard gives the sauce a special flavor, but it has to be thickened for at least 10 minutes.

■ The fillet is done when it reaches a core temperature of 170°F (78°C). Let rest for at least 5 minutes so that the meat juices can spread and the pork fillet becomes even more tender **(5)**.

■ Potatoes or noodles are excellent as a side dish.

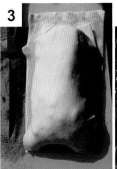

Ingredients (serves 4)

1 lb. (500g)	pork tenderloin

Marinade ────────

5 tbsp.	olive oil
5 tbsp.	lemon juice
1/2 tbsp.	juniper berries, crushed
1 tbsp.	oregano
	salt
	pepper

Preparation

■ Mix the olive oil and lemon juice with the crushed juniper berries, oregano, salt, and pepper to form a marinade.

■ According to the size of the pork tenderloin, cut the meat into pieces that are as thick as a finger and place in the marinade in a sealable plastic bag for at least 3 hours — best overnight **(1)**.

■ Slide the fillet pieces on metal or soaked wooden skewers so that the cut surface of the fillet lies on the grill **(2)**.

■ Grill for approximately 3 minutes on all sides and serve hot.

■ Fresh tzatziki (Greek cucumber yogurt dip) makes an excellent dip for this dish.

This dish is very well suited to feed a large number of guests because it is easy to prepare and gets better the later the guests arrive.

Ingredients (serves 6)

2	pork tenderloins
1 lb. (400g)	smoked bacon slices
4 cups	cream
1/3 cup (8cl)	tomato paste
8 cans	tomatoes
1 tbsp.	rosemary, chopped
2 tbsp.	basil, chopped
1 tbsp.	thyme
3	garlic cloves
16 oz.	red wine
some	butter

Preparation

■ Take out the tendons of the pork tenderloins and remove the silver membrane. Certainly a butcher you trust will also do it for you. Cut the meat into pieces as thick as a finger.

■ Wrap the tenderloin pieces with the bacon slices. Make sure that all pieces of bone and rind are removed from the bacon. Based on the size of the meat, use two slices of bacon and place the finished pieces into the oven (**1**).

■ For the sauce, put the tomatoes in a container and liquefy with an immersion blender, and then pour into a pot that is as high as possible so you don't fill your kitchen with tomato splashes from the cooking sauce. Add the cream, wine, and spices and let thicken for at least 45 minutes. Season once more. The sauce must have a fairly thick consistency because in the oven some of the liquid will boil away.

■ Pour the hot sauce in the oven over the prepared pieces of meat. Add a few clumps of butter on top and cook for 45 to 60 minutes with a lot of top heat. After this time, enough flavor from the bacon is in the sauce and transferred into the pork fillet (**2**).

■ Every type of noodle goes wonderfully with this dish.

Ingredients (serves 4-5)

1 lb. (500g)	raw leberkäs mixture (see below)
10-1/2 oz. (300g)	raw smoked bratwurst, coarse
5 oz. (150g)	gouda or Emmentaler cheese
2	eggs
3	gouda or Emmentaler cheese slices
7 oz. (200g)	Black Forest ham slices
2 slices	toast or white bread
3	gherkin pickles

Leberkäs (literally "liver loaf") is a traditional German dish: Finely grind together 1/3 lb. each of lean beef and pork, and mix with 1/4 lb. medium-ground bacon, 1/2 tsp salt, 1/2 tsp white pepper, and enough ice water to make the mixture smooth. Add a half onion, peeled and grated, and a dash of marjoram.

Preparation

▪ Put the raw leberkäs mixture in a large bowl. Cut open the bratwurst and squeeze the filling into the bowl, and then dice the cheese, split the white bread into small pieces, and mix all ingredients well with a spoon.

▪ Hard-boil the eggs. Cut the eggs and gherkins into thin slices.

▪ Rub a loaf pan or aluminum pan with some oil and layer the edge all around with the ham slices. Let the ends extend over the baking dish edge.

▪ Spread a layer of the meat mixture evenly on the base of the baking dish and cover with egg slices (**1**).

▪ Now, fill in a second layer of the meat mixture and spread evenly. When the dish is filled to the top edge, place the cheese slices on top, garnish with the gherkin slices, and fold up the overlapping ham strips (**2**).

▪ Heat the wood-fired oven with small beech wood pieces to 430°F (220°C). If the rising heat is initially too high, cool down the firebricks with some cold water if necessary.

▪ Place the pan initially covered with some aluminum foil into the oven. As soon as the formation of smoke is no longer present, the dish can be uncovered. Bake for 45 to 55 minutes.

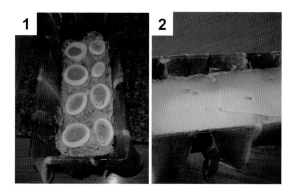

Beef

Ingredients (1 serving)

1   premium quality porterhouse
3   rosemary sprigs
3   garlic cloves
    salt
    pepper
    sugar
    olive oil

Preparation

■ Remove the steak from the refrigerator and bring to room temperature.

■ Prepare the grill for direct grilling and apply a cast iron grate.

■ Season the steak with salt, pepper, and sugar, and grill each side for six minutes at high heat. After three minutes, turn 90 degrees to get a nice grill pattern.

■ Preheat a pan with olive oil, garlic, and rosemary to 210°F (100°C).

■ After grilling, place the steak into the pan and let rest at 210°F (100°C) for five minutes with repeated turning.

■ Rosemary potatoes are excellent as a side dish.

Just **Steak**

For a good steak, you basically do not need a recipe, but rather instructions. A steak should be convincing by its meat flavor and not be adulterated by dominating sauces or marinades. The breed, origin, feeding method and slaughtering of the animal, maturation, storage, and, finally, the cut and type of the meat play a very large role in the later result, but are not heavily influential.

The first step for the average Joe — and at the same time the most important that leads to success — is the correct material selection. The best steaks for brief cooking are cut from the loin, the so-called prime cuts. The most popular here are certainly the rib eye/entrecote, roast beef/rump steak, t-bone, porterhouse, fillet, and haunch. Each piece, each cut has its own characteristic. From natural to finc, intensely flavorful to rather simple: lean meat without marbling will never offer the intense meat flavor like evenly marbled meat.

Marbling is the fine veins of fat that run through the meat. The more that can be seen, the more tender and juicier the final product will be. It is thus regarded that the fat brings the flavor. Therefore, you should, if necessary, cut it off just after grilling.

If you have bought a nice steak (1" or 3cm thickness is a good amount), you can follow the following instructions well:

■ Bring the meat to room temperature before grilling, never place cold meat on the grill.

■ Lightly oil the steak and season both sides with pepper.

■ Bring the grill to the highest possible temperature.

■ Apply the meat and grill for 1-1/2 minutes.

■ Turn 90 degrees and grill for an additional 1-1/2 minutes.

■ Turn with tongs.

■ Grill the other side for 3 minutes.

■ Wrap in aluminum foil and let rest for 10 minutes.

■ Season with coarse salt and fresh black pepper. Possibly enjoy with some horseradish.

The grilling times are for 1" thick (3cm) and nicely marbled steak, which should be grilled medium.

Ingredients (serves 4)

1	brisket with high fat content
5 tbsp.	brown sugar
5 tbsp.	paprika powder
1 tbsp.	cayenne pepper, ground
1 tbsp.	garlic powder
1 tbsp.	onion salt
2 tbsp.	black pepper, ground
1 tbsp.	sea salt
1 tbsp.	ginger powder
1 tbsp.	coriander, ground

Mop Sauce

2 cups (500ml)	apple juice or apple cider
2 tbsp.	brown sugar
1	onion
2 tbsp.	paprika powder

Preparation

■ Mix the spices well and rub the brisket with them.

■ Marinate the brisket in the refrigerator for at least 12, but preferably 24, hours.

■ The brisket must be removed from the refrigerator at least three hours before smoking so that it comes to room temperature.

■ Smoke for approximately 12 to 15 hours at a low temperature, between 210-250°F (100-120°C), until the meat has reached a core temperature of at least 195°F (90°C).

■ For the marinade, mix the apple juice (or apple cider), sugar, an onion cut into small rings, and the paprika powder. Brush the brisket with a mop brush or silicone brush for the first time after approximately 5 hours and then every 30 minutes.

■ When the core temperature of 195°F (90°C) has been reached, remove the meat from the smoker, wrap in aluminum foil, and let rest for 20 minutes.

Burgers

Ingredients (serves 6)

1 lb. (500g)	ground beef
2	tomatoes
1	large Spanish onion
5	pickles
	various sauces
	mustard
	individually wrapped cheese slices
6	large iceberg lettuce leaves
10 slices	bacon, cut somewhat thick
	mayonnaise
3 tbsp.	buller
6	hamburger rolls

Preparation

■ Have a small dish ready for each garnishing. Cut the tomatoes into slices and place in a container; also cut the pickles lengthwise in slices.

■ Divide the meat into six even portions. With somewhat moist hands, form a round, evenly thick hamburger out of each portion. To maintain the taste of the fresh beef, only slightly season with salt and pepper at the end (1).

■ Render the bacon in a cast iron pan until it is crispy and set aside. Brown the onion slices in the pan with the bacon grease.

■ Oil the hot grill grate so that the burgers do not stick.

■ Place the burgers on the hot grate and grill for 3 minutes on each side. Now they are done medium (2).

■ Spread 2 tbsp. of butter on the cut sides of the hamburger rolls and grill together with the buttered side facing down for the last 30 seconds. Careful, they become dark quickly (3)!

■ Place the burgers and the onion slices on top, add toppings as desired, and serve the burgers hot.

1

2

3

MEAT / BEEF

111

Tri-Tip Steak

Ingredients (serves 6)

1	tri-tip steak
2	onions
1 cup	basic rub
2 cups	orange juice

Tip
When the meat feels nicely tender with a simple hand test, it is done.

Preparation

■ Season the steak on all sides with the rub and marinate for at least 12, but preferably 24, hours.

■ Preheat the smoker to 210°F (100°C) and place the meat on for approximately 6 hours.

■ For the mop sauce, cut the onions into rings and put in a pot with the orange juice and 2 tbsp. of the rub and let everything simmer for 10 minutes.

■ After 2 hours, brush the meat with the mop sauce for the first time. After another hour, turn the meat and coat again with the mop sauce. Repeat every hour, making sure that the temperature in the smoker does not exceed 210°F (100°C).

■ Cut the meat against the grain and serve.

■ BBQ sauce or a fresh salad goes wonderfully well with this dish.

Blackened Rib Eye Steak

Ingredients (serves 4)

4	rib eye steaks, approximately 1" thick
	butter
	Paul Prudhomme's Blackened Steak Magic® Seasoning

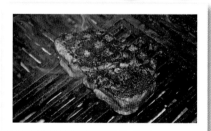

Preparation

■ Bring the grill to a high temperature with Heat Beads® for direct grilling.

■ Brush the cooled rib eye steaks with liquid butter. Let the butter cool and sprinkle the steaks with the blackened steak seasoning.

■ Directly grill each side for 2-1/2 minutes at the highest heat.

■ French fries and tomato salad go well with this dish.

Ingredients (serves 4)

14 oz. (400g)	tri-tip steak
1	red pepper
1 bunch	scallions
2	tomatoes
1	leak
2	chilies
1	red onion
4	fajitas
	sea salt

Dip

1 tbsp.	tomato paste
1 cup	sour cream
2 tbsp.	sambal oelek (chili-based sauce)

Preparation

■ Remove the seeds from the pepper and divide into eight pieces, clean the leek and scallions, and cut the tomatoes into slices. Grill the vegetables well on all sides and then cut into small cubes of approximately 3/4" (2cm).

■ For the dip, mix the sour cream, tomato paste, and sambal oelek in a bowl until a smooth mixture forms.

■ Briefly brown the fajitas in a pan.

■ Season the meat with pepper and grill both sides for three minutes and then remove from the grill. Season with sea salt and let rest in aluminum foil for five minutes.

■ In the meantime, coat the fajitas with the dip and top with the grilled vegetables. Cut the meat into thin slices and also place on the fajitas. Roll up the fajitas and servc.

Churrasco with Ramsons Chimichurri

Ingredients (serves 4)

2	fillets of beef, center cuts, approximately 6" long (15cm)

Marinade

1 large bunch	ramsoms (wild garlic)
1 large bunch	flat-leaf parsley
1/2 cup (150ml)	extra virgin olive oil
1/3 cup (100ml)	sunflower oil
1 oz. (30ml)	balsamic vinegar
3 tbsp.	water
2 tsp.	sea salt
1 tsp.	tellicherry pepper, coarsely ground

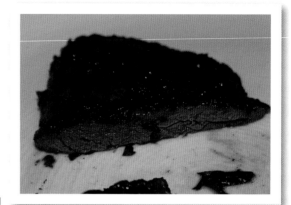

Preparation

■ Cut the fillet pieces along the grain into four slices and carefully harmonize with the meat tenderizer.

■ Finely chop the herbs; mix well with the remaining ingredients, but do not completely emulsify.

■ Set aside half of the marinade in a cool place. Marinate the fillet slices with the other half and let rest in the refrigerator for one hour or longer.

■ Directly grill the drained fillet slices on a cast iron grate for 2 minutes on each side at maximum heat. Turn the fillets 90 degrees after 1 minute to keep a nice grill pattern.

■ Preheat the oven with the top and bottom heat at 175°F (80°C). Keep the fillet warm in the preheated oven until serving and then pour on the remaining marinade. Serve immediately.

■ Tomatoes and shallots mixed with cheese and herbs, as well as fried tomatoes and herbed cottage cheese, go very well with this dish.

Tip
Sealable plastic bags have proven to be extremely practical for marinating. They are very easy to open and close with the help of a slide, and in contrast to bowls you save a large amount of marinade because the grill food is completely surrounded by the marinade and can be stored airtight.

Prime Rib au Jus

Ingredients (serves 6)

1	prime rib of beef with bone, approximately 7-1/2 lbs. (3.5kg)
1 quart	beef bouillon
1 cup (200ml)	red wine
3	onions
3 stalks	celery
2	parsley roots
2	garlic cloves
14 oz. (400g)	mushrooms
2 tbsp.	sunflower oil
1 tbsp.	starch
	pepper
	salt

Preparation

■ For the jus, dice the onions, celery, root parsley, garlic, and mushrooms and saute until brown in oil.

■ Add red wine and cook until the wine has nearly evaporated (1).

■ Add the bouillon, bring to a boil, and reduce to half to a meat stock. Pour through a fine sieve, season with salt and pepper, and thicken with starch that has dissolved in cold water. Keep warm.

■ Season the prime rib with salt and pepper and cook in a smoker that is fired by beech or fruit wood to a temperature of 230-265°F (110-130°C) until the meat has reached a core temperature of 120-125°F (48-50°C). Wrap the meat in aluminum foil and let rest in a warm spot for 30 minutes, and then carve and serve au jus (2).

■ Small green peppers (3) with coarse sea salt fried in olive oil and baked potatoes with herbed cottage cheese go excellent with this dish.

Fillet of Beef
with Spinach Shrimp and Chanterelles

Ingredients (serves 4)

4	fillet of beef steaks, 1/2" to 2" thick (4-5cm)
4	small shrimp
	garlic
	leaf spinach for wrapping
8 slices	Serrano or Parma ham
	salt
	pepper
14 oz. (400g)	chanterelle mushrooms
1/2 bunch	flat leaf parsley
3	shallots
	oil

Preparation

■ Cut off the heads of the shrimp, peel, and skewer lengthwise on a toothpick so that they don't become crooked during blanching.

■ Blanch the shrimps for 1 minute, the spinach for 10 seconds.

■ Remove the stems from the leaf spinach and spread out on a board. Season with little garlic and pepper and then wrap around the shrimp.

■ With a knife, make a hole lengthwise through the fillet and widen to the thickness of the shrimp. Twist the shrimp into the fillet — against the winding of the spinach — until it is in the center of the fillet (1).

■ Wrap the stuffed meat crosswise in the ham, whereby the second layer of ham should correspond to the direction of the shrimp. This later serves as the cutting guide.

■ Directly grill the meat for 90 seconds each on both sides at high temperature on the griddle and then in-directly for 6 minutes at 320-360°F (160-180°C) until done. Let rest in aluminum foil for 5 minutes.

■ Wash and clean the chanterelles. Finely dice the shallots, chop the parsley.

■ Heat oil in a pan and brown the chanterelles in it. Add the shallots and parsley and fry everything for approximately 5 to 7 minutes.

■ Cut the fillets diagonally to the second piece of ham so that the cut the cut runs crosswise through the shrimp.

■ Season with salt and pepper to taste and serve.

1

Ingredients (serves 8)

3-1/2 lbs. (1.6kg)	roast beef
6	shallots, finely diced
4	garlic cloves, finely minced
4 tsp.	tomato paste
1-3/4 cups (400ml)	dry red wine
1 liter	veal stock
2 tsp.	red or green peppercorns, pickled
8 tbsp.	balsamic vinegar
10-1/2 oz. (300g)	butter
	salt from the mill
	pepper from the mill
	starch for binding
	caramel for coloring

Preparation

■ Blot dry and trim the roast beef. In the process, do not remove the white layer of fat.

■ Sear as a whole on all sides in a preheated roasting pan.

■ Remove the meat from the roasting pan and indirectly grill on the grill at 320°F (160°C) until a core temperature of 130-135°F (54-56°C) has been reached.

■ For the sauce, add the tomato paste to the drippings and braise the shallots and garlic in it. Add the red wine and reduce to approximately 1/4 of the amount.

■ Add the veal stock and reduce everything to approximately 2-1/2 cups (600ml) and then sieve.

■ Rinse the peppercorn under lukewarm water and add to the sauce with the balsamic vinegar.

■ Stir in the butter in clumps and season with salt and pepper.

■ When the core temperature has been reached, remove from the grill and let rest in aluminum foil for 15 minutes.

■ Cut into slices for serving and sprinkle with salt and pepper.

■ Collect the escaping meat juice and add to the sauce.

Tip

With roast beef, like with nearly all meat products, the typical meat flavor is reached only by the quality of the product. Here there is special attention of a distinct marbling. A lean piece will never achieve the flavor of a finely marbled piece. Do not remove the fat before grilling but rather cut away afterwards according to preference.

Ingredients (serves 6)

4 lbs. (2kg)	braised beef
2-3	garlic cloves, sliced
2-3 tbsp.	oil
1-2	carrots, julienned
2	onions, diced
1	small cabbage, diced
2 stalks	celery, diced
	pepper
	salt
6-7	cloves
1 bottle	dry red wine
1 can	peeled tomatoes
1 qt (1.2 l)	meat broth
7 oz. (200g)	pecorino (Italian cheese)
	nutmeg
12	large cannelloni
2 cups	béchamel (white) sauce
7 oz. (200g)	grated cheese

Tip

With this recipe you get two complete meals and lots of delicious sauce for more use. Do not remove the fat before grilling but rather cut away afterwards according to preference.

Preparation

■ Peel the garlic cloves and cut into small slices. Score the meat all around with a knife and lard with garlic.

■ Brown well all around in some grease or oil.

■ Add the carrots, onions, celery, and cabbage, and brown. Season with salt and pepper and add the cloves. Add a bottle of red wine and reduce slightly.

■ Add the peeled tomatoes and season again. Now, gradually add approximately 1 quart of meat broth.

■ Cook everything at medium heat in the roaster for 3 hours.

■ Press the sauce through a sieve and season again if necessary.

■ Approximately half of the braised beef can now be consumed directly hot. The other half is further used in the cannelloni filling.

■ Let approximately 2 lbs. (1kg) of the braised beef cool, cut into pieces, and mince in a meat grinder with a large disc. Brown the meat filling in some oil; grate the pecorino cheese and mix in. Season with pepper, salt, and nutmeg.

■ Now fill the cannelloni and lay next to each other in a baking dish. Pour the béchamel (white) sauce on top, add some of the remaining roast sauce, and sprinkle with a grated cheese of your choice.

■ Heat the wood-fired oven with beech wood to approximately 395°F (200°C) and bake the cannelloni for approximately 30 minutes.

Ingredients (serves 2)

14 oz. (400g)	top butt flap (sirloin tip)
	salt
	pepper
	sugar
	sea salt

Salsa

3	tomatoes
1/2	pink grapefruit
1/2	mango
1/2	red onion
2	garlic cloves
2 tbsp.	coriander leaves
1	red chili pepper, fresh
1 tsp.	paprika powder, sweet
1/2 tsp.	cumin, ground
1 pinch	cardamom, ground
2 tbsp.	olive oil
1 shot	wine vinegar
	salt
	pepper

Preparation

■ For the salsa, skin the tomatoes, peel the mango, fillet the grapefruit, and dice everything. Dice the onions and garlic and mix all ingredients. Season with salt and pepper and marinate for at least 2 hours in the refrigerator.

■ Season the top butt flap with salt, pepper, and a pinch of sugar.

■ Prepare the grill for direct grilling and grill the meat for 2 minutes on each side at high heat.

■ Let the meat briefly rest, then slice, and season with some sea salt. Serve together with the salsa.

Old English **Beer Casserole**

Ingredients (serves 4-6)

21 oz. (600g)	veal from the knuckle or beef
1 lb. (500g)	mushrooms
1/2 cup	flour
2	garlic cloves
1	large onion
3	bay leaves
1 bottle	dark beer
1 cup (300ml)	meat broth
1/2 lb (200g)	bacon
one shot	vinegar

Preparation

■ Cut the meat in 3/4" to 1" large cubes (2-3cm).

■ Briefly sear the meat on the lid of the Dutch oven then let rest in the Dutch oven **(1)**.

■ Lightly sauté the chopped bacon and diced onions. Add the crushed garlic cloves, flour, and bay leaves.

■ Pour the beer and meat broth on top and mix well. Make sure that a darkest possible beer or wheat beer is used. The dish becomes very bitter with pilsner and other types of pale beers **(2)**.

■ Cook with a lot of top heat for 1 hour and season with vinegar before serving **(3)**.

■ Bread dumplings go well as a side dish and for a drink you should serve the same beer that you used for cooking.

Ingredients (serves 4)

4	rib steaks, approximately 1 lb.(500g) each
4	small red peppers
10	mild peppers
3	scallions
5	shallots
2	small zucchinis
12	cherry tomatoes
15	small new potatoes
2	sweet potatoes
	bay leaf, sage, rosemary, parsley
	pepper, coarse sea salt
	beef marrow bones
	herbed cottage cheese

Preparation

■ Peel the shallots and cut into halves, and then clean the scallions and cut into large pieces. Put both in a stainless steel roaster that fits between the charcoal trays of a kettle grill.

■ Wash the paprika, peppers, zucchini, and cherry tomatoes and also place whole into the roaster. Work in coarsely plucked parsley (1).

■ Clean the new potatoes and sweet potatoes and then add whole with coarsely plucked bay leaf, sage, and rosemary to the vegetables. Season with freshly ground pepper and coarse sea salt (2).

■ Set the roaster in the grill between the charcoal. Put the grill grate on top and place a few beef marrowbones over the vegetables. Indirectly grill for approximately 90 minutes with a closed lid.

■ Occasionally turn the bones until the potatoes brown. The liquid marrow drips into the vegetables and gives them an excellent flavor (3).

■ Lightly oil the steaks.

■ Remove the vegetables from the grill and keep warm.

■ Push together the charcoal baskets in the grill center for direct grilling and heat an oiled cast iron grate.

■ Directly grill the steaks for 3 minutes on each side with a closed lid. Turn the meat 90 degrees after approximately 1-1/2 minutes.

■ Serve herbed cottage cheese with the vegetables.

Bulgogi

The dish is also known by the name "Korean fire meat." Thin strips of beef, less frequently pork, are marinated and then grilled at the table. It is regarded as a festive meal. Traditionally, it is prepared in a charcoal grill. In specialized restaurants, the tables are provided with gas operated or electric grill plates.

Ingredients (serves 4)

1 lb. (500g)	beef tenderloin or fillet
1	garlic clove
1	apple
1	pear
8 tbsp.	soy sauce
1	thumb-sized piece of ginger or ginger powder
2 tbsp.	sesame oil
2 tbsp.	wine or sake
1	onion
3 tbsp.	brown sugar
1 tsp.	pepper

For the Rice Dish _____

18 oz. (500g)	rice (2 pouches)
1/2 lb. (250g)	oyster mushrooms
2 tbsp.	sesame oil
1	bell pepper

Tip

Naturally this dish can be prepared on every traditional grill. However, it is more sociable when it is directly cooked on the table. It is ideal if you own a table grill. Otherwise, at your next hardware store visit, check to see if there are any cheap folding grills. They are easy and quickly put together and ready to be used on every table. As a precaution, place a stone plate underneath to avoid burn marks on the table.

Preparation

■ Have the meat cut by the butcher in 1/8"-thick (2-3mm) slices.

■ For the marinade, put the sugar, sesame oil, soy sauce, pepper, wine, and pressed garlic in a bowl. Peel the apple, pear, ginger, and onion; grate, and add. Place the beef in a bag and pour the marinade on top. Marinate for at least 1 hour **(1)**.

■ Cook two pouches of rice until they *al dente*. Now, cut the pepper and mushrooms into strips and briefly brown in sesame oil. Add in a 1"-long (3cm) piece of grated ginger and brown together, and then add the hot rice. Briefly stir. Season with salt and pepper **(2)**.

■ Prepare the usual amount of charcoal in the charcoal starter and then place it into the grill.

■ Because the meat is cut very thin, the meat is cooked within a few seconds. If it is exposed to the heat for too long, it will become dry and tough. Try first with one piece and check the result before you apply the other pieces of meat **(3)**.

■ Each guest can place many slices on the grill with a fork or grill tongs as they like and grill as desired.

Meat Loaf

Ingredients (serves 4-6)

2 lbs. (1kg)	ground beef
	Tabasco, green or red
1	carrot
1	onion
1	egg
2	hamburger rolls or the like
1/2 tsp.	pepper
1 tsp.	chili powder
1 tsp.	thyme
1-1/2 tsp.	salt
2	garlic cloves

Glaze

1/2 cup	ketchup
1 tbsp.	cumin
1 tbsp.	Worcestershire sauce
1 tbsp.	honey
1 tbsp.	Tabasco

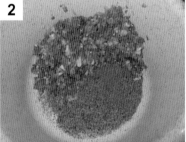

Preparation

■ Crisp the hamburger rolls in the oven (or on second grill).

■ Put the chili powder, thyme, salt, and pepper into the food processor. Cut up the rolls, add, and finely grind everything (**1**).

■ Place the powder and pepper into a sturdy bowl. Chop the onion, carrot, and garlic into pieces that aren't too small and mix in (**2**).

■ Add the egg and ground beef into the bowl; mix very carefully with as little force as possible (**3**).

■ Form a loaf from the mixture, slightly press, and place on a base that is as thin as possible, such as a glass tray (**4**).

■ Now heat up the grill. Make sure that you only work with indirect heat here. The briquettes (approximately a chimney starter full) are placed to the left and right in the kettle grill. In the center, position a stainless steel drip pan filled with water.

■ Let the meat loaf slide from the glass tray onto the oiled grate. Stick a meat thermometer into the meat at a 45° angle; make sure that the thermometer does not go into the meat too deeply and the tip is precisely in the center of the loaf (**5**).

■ To get a nice crust, the meat loaf has to be glazed: for this, combine ketchup, honey, Worcestershire sauce, cumin, and Tabasco. Depending on how hot the glaze should be, either use the milder, green Tabasco or the hotter, red Tabasco. Stir well and, after 10 minutes in the grill, brush the loaf on all sides (**6**).

■ The meat loaf is done when the core temperature of 145°F (63°C) has been reached.

■ Slide the loaf along the running direction of the grill grate back onto the cleaned glass tray.

■ Let the loaf rest for at least 5, preferably 10, minutes so that the meat becomes more tender and juicier.

■ Coleslaw goes well with this dish.

Tips

Aluminum trays can be used as drip pans, but they are difficult to clean. In every large supermarket, stainless steel or glass trays that fit perfectly in your grill are available inexpensively.

If you do not have a thermometer, you can remove the meat loaf from the grill after approximately 70 minutes. However, the core temperature can greatly differ because it is dependent on many factors:

1. Thickness of the loaf

2. Amount of charcoal or briquettes

3. The more often you lift the lid, the longer the cooking time becomes because each time the heat escapes. Here a control of curiosity is sensible. You will see that nothing can go wrong.

4. Also make sure that the ventilation slides at the top and bottom are open so that an air draft can develop that brings fresh oxygen into the grill. Otherwise the charcoal can go out.

This dish is ideally prepared for guests. You should preferably cook too much of it because frozen in portions it results in a prepared feast in minutes for a busy weekday.

Ingredients (serves 4-6)

2 lbs (1kg)	veal
1	red pepper
1/2	yellow pepper
1	carrot
1-1/2 qt (1.5 l)	meat broth
3	medium-sized onions
1	garlic clove
3 tbsp.	paprika powder
1 tbsp.	chili powder
1 tsp.	salt
1 tsp.	pepper
1	large can of tomatoes
1 tsp.	thyme
2 containers	cream
3 tbsp.	flour
1 cup	red wine
6 tbsp.	tomato paste

Preparation

■ Have the veal chopped up by your butcher or cut it yourself to the desired size. Without searing, place in the oven. For the above mentioned amount a 12" large, flat pot is suitable.

■ Chop the peppers, onions, and carrot, crush the garlic, and cut the tomatoes into pieces that aren't too big.

■ Pour the cream, meat broth, and wine on top, mix in the spices and flour, and cook with as much top heat as possible and high bottom heat for 70 minutes with a closed lid.

■ Noodles or dumplings go well with this dish. If you prefer this to be especially authentic, serve bread dumplings as a side dish.

Ingredients (serves 4)

1 lb. (500g)	ground beef
4	burger rolls
2	shallots
1	orange
2 tbsp.	truffle butter (or 1 tsp. truffle oil)
3-1/2 tbsp. (50g)	sun-dried tomatoes in oil
	old balsamic vinegar
1	truffle
4	slices of brie cheese
	arugula
	salt
	pepper

Preparation

■ Finely dice the shallots and lightly sauté in the truffle butter. Dice the sun-dried tomatoes and add. Add the orange zest and juice, pour some old balsamic vinegar on top, and reduce at medium heat.

■ Divide the ground meat into 4 even portions. With slightly moist hands, form a round, evenly thick burger out of each portion and season with salt and pepper.

■ Directly grill the burgers for approximately 2-1/2 minutes on each side.

■ Cut open the rolls and place on the grill for 1 minute with the cut sides facing down.

■ Put the reduced balsamic sauce on the burger rolls. Clean the arugula and put on the bottom burger roll half. Then put a burger on top and then a slice of brie. Finally, slice a truffle on top.

Ingredients

All variants for 4 people

Preparation

■ Puree the avocados to make guacamole.

■ Grill the bell pepper and chili, and then skin the pepper (**1**).

■ Sear the meat and onions that are cut into rough slices in portions. Add the pepper and briefly cook together (**2**).

■ Warm the wheat tortillas in the oven. Spread the cooked ingredients with guacamole and possibly some cheese on top; now, carefully roll the tortillas (**3**).

■ Serve with Spanish rice.

1

2

3

Variant 1: Fajitas with Beef

3-4 lb	bottom round steak cut in thin strips
1/2	onion, coarsely cut
2	garlic cloves, minced
3 tbsp.	oil
1 tbsp.	soy sauce
1 tsp.	liquid smoke
1 tsp.	coriander
	cumin, according to taste
1 tbsp.	Worcestershire sauce
1 tbsp.	brown sugar
	ground chili, according to taste
2	avocados
4	wheat tortillas

Variant 2: Fajitas with Chicken

4	chicken breast fillets
2	garlic cloves, minced
3 tbsp.	lime juice
1 tbsp.	coriander
3 tbsp.	Worcestershire sauce
	cumin
3/4 tbsp.	granulated chicken broth
2	avocados
4	wheat tortillas

Variant 3: Fajitas with Beef and Chicken

2 lbs	bottom round steak cut in thin strips
2	chicken breast fillets
1/2	onion, coarsely cut
2	garlic cloves, minced
4 tbsp.	oil
2 tsp.	basil
2 tsp.	coriander
1 tsp.	thyme
	paprika
	salt, pepper
1 tbsp.	soy sauce
2	avocados
4	wheat tortillas

MEAT / BEEF

129

Ingredients (serves 6)

3 lbs. (1.5kg)	beef, cubed
2 lbs. (1kg)	(Spanish) onions
3	bell pepper
1	tomato
1	chili
1	pepperoncini
1/2 lb. (250g)	mushrooms
1/2 liter	pinot noir
	salt
	pepper
	paprika seasoning, sweet
	sugar
	mustard seed
	beef suet

Preparation

■ Cube the beef, cut the onions into half rings, cut the bell pepper, tomato, chili, and pepperoncini into small strips, and clean the fresh mushrooms.

■ Mix the salt, pepper, paprika seasoning, mustard seed, and some sugar.

■ Light 35 grill briquettes and place in the fireplace. Set the oven on top and render some beef suet.

■ Add all of the beef and then the mushrooms, onions, spices, pepper and chili strips, and tomato. Pour the red wine on top and cover with the lid (1).

■ Place approximately half of the charcoal on the lid (2).

■ Cook for approximately 2-1/2 hours. Season again and serve hot (3).

1

2

3

MEAT / BEEF

Lamb

Ingredients (serves 4)

8   lamb chops
8   garlic cloves
    black pepper, coarsely ground
    herb oil
    herbs according to preference
    salt

Preparation

■ Wash the lamb chops and blot dry (1).

■ Peel the garlic cloves, cut into thin strips, and lard the chops with it.

■ Rub the meat with the pepper and coat with the herb oil and herbs.

■ Grill the lamb chops on the hot grill for six to eight minutes, turning once and salting lightly just before serving (2).

Lamb Knuckles

Ingredients (serves 6)

6	lamb knuckles
3 tsp.	fresh rosemary
3 tsp.	fresh thyme
3 tsp.	fresh oregano
2 tsp.	black pepper, coarsely ground
3	garlic cloves, finely minced
	olive oil
1/2 liter	white wine
10	small potatoes
2	zucchinis
2	carrots
	lard

Preparation

■ Remove the skin and fat from the knuckles as well as possible.

■ Finely chop the herbs and mix with the garlic and pepper. Add some olive oil and spread the marinade on the knuckles. Marinate in the refrigerator for 24 hours.

■ Peel the vegetables and potatoes and coarsely cut into pieces. Grease a roaster with some lard and layer the vegetables inside. Season with salt and pepper and pour white wine on top **(1)**.

■ Place a grill grate in the roaster on the vegetables.

■ Wipe the marinade from the knuckles and place the knuckles on the grate **(2)**.

■ Pre-heat the wood-fired oven to 480°F (250°C), insert the roaster with a closed lid, and cook for 45 minutes with decreasing heat.

■ Then remove the lid from the roaster and brown the knuckles for 15 to 20 minutes at 320-340°F (160-170°C) **(3)**.

■ Serve 1 to 2 knuckles with some vegetables on a plate and serve hot.

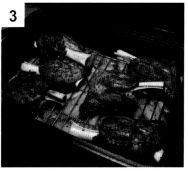

Ingredients (serves 6)

4-1/2 lbs. (2kg)	boneless leg of lamb
2	garlic cloves, cut into slices
2 tsp.	fresh thyme
2 tsp.	fresh rosemary, chopped
2 tsp.	black pepper, coarsely ground
	salt
	clarified butter
1-3/4 cup (400ml)	lamb stock
1 cup (250ml)	Madeira, medium sweet
3	medium-sized onions, cut into quarters
5	bay leaves
3-1/2 oz. (100g)	sun-dried tomatoes
3-1/2 oz. (100g)	black olives
1	unwaxed lemon, cut into eighths
1 handful	coriander herb, coarsely plucked
1 handful	parsley, plucked

Preparation

■ Remove the fat and tendons from the inside of the leg. Cut small pockets into the outer fat layer with a pointed knife. Cut the garlic into slices and insert into the pockets. Mix the herbs with salt and rub the leg all around with it.

■ Heat up the wood-fired oven. In an iron pan or roaster, melt some butter and cook the leg in the oven on both sides until golden brown (1).

■ If necessary, rearrange the leg in the roaster and pour the lamb stock and Madeira on top.

■ Braise the onions in an iron pan and with the bay leaf add to the leg of lamb. Close the roaster with the lid and let braise at 355°F (180°C) for 2 hours (2).

■ After two hours, add the sun-dried tomatoes, olives, lemon wedges, coriander herb, and parsley to the meat and place the roaster in the oven for an additional 30 minutes (3).

■ Cut the leg into slices and serve with the sauce.

■ Rosemary potatoes are excellent with this dish.

1 2 3

Ingredients (serves 6)

1 lb. (500g)	small onions
1-3/4 lb. (800g)	carrots
1/2 bulb	fennel
1	small bulb of garlic
1 bunch	celery, without leaves
2	lamb shoulders, 2 lbs. (1kg) each
	clarified butter
	pepper
	salt
1 large pinch	caraway seed
2 cups (1/2 l)	dark beer
2 cups (1/2 l)	lamb stock
1 tbsp.	syrup

Preparation

- Coarsely chop the vegetables.

- Pre-heat an iron pan with olive oil and brown the shoulders on both sides **(1)**.

- Transfer the shoulders into a roaster and thoroughly season with salt and pepper.

- Lightly sauté the vegetables — except for the fennel — in the pan one after the other and slightly brown.

- Layer the vegetables and fennel in the roaster, and then pour the dark beer and the lamb stock on top **(2)**.

- Braise with a closed lid for 2 hours in the wood-fired oven at 360°F (180°C).

- Take the meat and vegetables from the roaster. Slightly reduce the remaining sauce, mix in the syrup, and, if required, bind slightly **(3)**.

- Fold the vegetables into the sauce.

- Serve some of the sauce with vegetables on a plate, cut the shoulders into slices, and place on top of the vegetables.

Ingredients (serves 25)

1	whole lamb (approximately 44 lbs. or 20kg)
4 cups	olive oil (1 liter)
1 cup	rosemary
1 cup	oregano
20	garlic cloves
3 tbsp.	pepper
3 tbsp.	salt
4 tbsp.	paprika, sweet

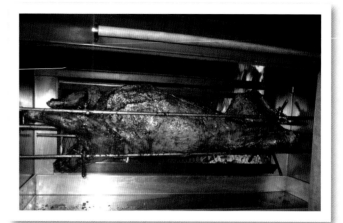

Preparation

■ Securely fasten the lamb on the rotisserie and light the grill. Note: The lamb must continuously be turned during the 7-hour cooking time.

■ Regularly coat the lamb with olive oil with a long brush.

■ After approximately 5 hours, add the spices to the olive oil and regularly thoroughly brush the lamb with them.

■ Before serving remove the lamb from the grill and carve on a table.

Tip

To grill an entire lamb, a "special frame-work" is required: Use a rotisserie with a hand crank or a professional rotisserie grill. It is important to secure the lamb well. Also, tie the legs and shoulders to the rotisserie with wire and secure the back with a clamp or wire before turning.

Sausage

Wild Garlic **Sausage**

Ingredients (serves 4)

2 lbs. (1kg)	pork neck
1 lb. (500g)	beef neck
2 lbs. (1kg)	pork belly
2-1/2 tbsp. (50g)	salt
2-1/2 tsp. (10g)	celery salt
3 tsp. (7.5g)	white pepper, ground
2 tsp. (2.5g)	thyme, dried
1 oz. (25g)	fresh parsley, chopped
1 oz. (25g)	fresh ramsons, chopped
1/2 tsp. (1.25g)	mace
	natural pork casing

Preparation

■ Dice the meat to the inlet size of the meat grinder.

■ Grind the beef neck and pork neck with a meat grinder with a hole size of 4.

■ Grind the pork belly with a meat grinder with a hole size of 2.

■ Combine the remaining ingredients with the meat **(1)**.

■ Soak the natural pork casing for 30 minutes in lukewarm water and then rinse well **(2)**.

■ Fill the sausage meat into the natural pork casing with a sausage stuffer. Twist off the sausage at a length of approximately 8" to 10" (20-25cm). Pierce any resulting air bubbles multiple times **(3)**.

■ Directly grill at medium heat until the sausages are fragrant, possibly brown according to taste.

1

2

3

Cevapcici (Sausage)

Ingredients (serves 4)

12 oz. (350g)	ground pork
2	garlic cloves
1/2 tsp.	salt
1/4 tsp.	black pepper
1 tbsp.	paprika powder
1 tbsp.	olive oil
1	onion
1/4	bell pepper

Preparation

■ Peel and finely dice the onion. Wash the pepper, blot dry, remove the seeds, and cut into strips. Peel the garlic cloves and crush with a press (1).

■ Work the ground meat together with the garlic, salt, pepper, and paprika powder into a dough using a hand mixer with dough hooks. With moist hands, form finger-long, 3/4" (2cm) thick sausages from the meat mixture (2).

■ Place the cevapcici next to each other on a dish, cover and marinate for 30 minutes in the refrigerator.

■ Cook the cevapcici at low to medium heat for approximately 5 minutes on each side until crispy. Careful, they become dark quickly!

■ Serve ajvar (relish) and tzatziki (sauce) with it. Djuvec rice (see page 197) is especially suited as a side dish.

Tip

Ajvar is a bell pepper or bell pepper-eggplant puree with a Serbian origin that serves as a cold spread or is served with meat. Traditionally prepared, red peppers are browned, skinned, seeded, and gently cooked with some oil with constant stirring until they have dissolved into a uniform mixture, which can take many hours. The only seasonings used are salt and pepper. Stored airtight, this ajvar keeps for a long time. Other ingredients can be added. For this, red peppers and eggplant are first roasted in the oven and peeled, the pepper is seeded, everything is finely chopped, mixed with olive oil and lemon juice or vinegar, chilies, garlic, pepper, salt, and finely diced, steamed onions, and gently cooked until the liquid is nearly boiled down.

1

2

Curried Sausage from the Grill

Curried sausage is a simple and quick dish that both the young and the old enjoy. Unfortunately, many times, when you order a curried sausage in restaurants, it only comes with mundane ketchup with some curry powder. Many guard their sauce recipe like gold, but basically it is very easy, and we are revealing the secret. You won't believe it, but the sauce no longer tastes like boring ketchup!

Ingredients (2 pieces per person)

Curried sausage or bockwurst

2 bottles	ketchup
1 tsp.	chili powder
3 tbsp.	Worcestershire sauce
3 tbsp.	soy sauce
1 can	meat broth
1 tbsp.	paprika, sweet

At least 2 tbsp. of curry, depending on the hotness of the powder.

Preparation

■ Cut the sausages crosswise on both sides at a distance of approximately 3/4" (2cm) and place on the grill. Cook 3 to 5 minutes on each side at medium heat.

■ For the sauce take your favorite ketchup and heat it slowly. Add the chili powder, Worcestershire sauce, soy sauce, meat broth, paprika powder, and, of course, the curry and mix well.

■ Pour the sauce on top of the sausages, sprinkle curry once more on top, and serve hot.

■ Fries or fried potatoes are an excellent side dish.

Smoking Sausages

Preparation

■ Take two sausages per person.

■ Pre-heat the wood-fired oven to 300°F (150°C); maintain this temperature for 20 minutes and then close the flue damper (1).

■ Remove the top stones, hang the lightly salted sausages in the oven, and throw a handful of smoking dust onto the heat source. Close the oven immediately and smoke the sausages for approximately 30 minutes with a slowly decreasing temperature (2, 3).

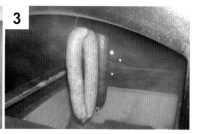

Fresh Grilled (Thuringian) Sausage

This recipe results in 40 to 50 sausages depending on the length of the sausage and casing diameter. Since sheet ribbed, rindless, boneless pork belly under 6-1/2 pounds (3kg) is difficult to obtain, sausages should be made with the above-mentioned amount.

Ingredients (serves 25)

6-1/2 lbs. (3kg)	pork: approximately 50% sheet ribbed, rindless, boneless pork belly and 50% pork neck (without bones and rind)
3 tbsp. (50g)	salt
1-1/2 tsp. (12g)	black pepper
1 tsp.	mace
2 tsp.	sugar
2 tsp.	marjoram, destemmed
1 tsp.	garlic, roasted
2 tsp.	onion granules
2 tsp. (7g)	whole yellow mustard seed
2 tsp. (7g)	caraway seed, not ground
3	eggs (size medium)
1-1/4 cup (300ml)	very cold whole milk
	pork small intestines

Preparation

■ Prepare the meat to the inlet size of the meat grinder and freeze for 1 hour.

■ Grind the meat at a hole size of 8.

■ Pulverize the salt, pepper, mace, sugar, marjoram, garlic, and onions, and mix with caraway seed and mustard. Gradually work the seasoning into the meat in portions.

■ Distribute the eggs and milk into the mixture and homogenize the sausage meat for 15 minutes with a kneading machine at low to medium speed.

■ Soak the pork small intestines for 30 minutes in lukewarm water and then rinse well.

■ Fill the sausage meat into the pork casings with a sausage stuffer with a 30/32 caliber. Twist off the

Tip
After immediate vacuuming and shrink-wrapping the storage time in the refrigerator amounts to a maximum of 3 days at under 40°F (5°C). To extend the preservability put the sausages in cold, salty vinegar water (1 tsp. salt and vinegar per liter of water) and blanch until boiling point. Then rinse with cold water, wash off, dry, cool down, and vacuum seal. Freeze for a maximum of 2 months.

sausage at a length of 8" to 10" (20-25cm). Pierce any resulting air bubbles multiple times.

■ Directly grill at medium heat until the sausages are fragrant, possibly brown according to taste.

■ Because Thuringian Bratwurst is very savory, a somewhat mild mustard and fresh roll go well with it.

MEAT / SAUSAGE

Thuringian **Cheese Sausage**

Ingredients (serves 4)

10-1/2 oz. (300g)	ground pork
1	egg
1	small roll or 1 slice of toast
1	large onion
7 oz. (200g)	cheese (gouda in one piece)
	bread crumbs
2	garlic cloves
1 tbsp.	mustard
1 tbsp.	marjoram
	pepper
	salt

Preparation

■ Mix the ground meat with the diced onion, chopped toast, minced garlic, marjoram, mustard, and egg, thoroughly season with salt and pepper.

■ Cut the cheese into approximately 2" (5cm) long strips **(1)**.

■ Form small sausages from the meat mixture and add a cheese strip to the center of each, tightly seal around **(2)**.

■ Roll the little sausages in bread crumbs and slowly cook on the grate with careful turning until a nice, light brown crust develops **(3)**.

■ This dish can also be prepared without bread crumbs.

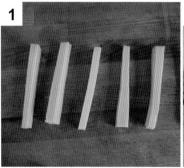

Fish

Ingredients (serves 6)

16	jumbo shrimp, peeled and de-veined
16	thin slices of breakfast bacon or Serrano ham
	metal skewers (if wooden skewers are used: soak in water)

Marinade

1 tbsp.	butter
1	small onion
6 oz. (180g)	ketchup
3 tbsp.	Worcestershire sauce
2 tbsp.	steak sauce
1 tbsp.	apple cider vinegar
3 tbsp.	brown sugar
1/4 cup	water (60ml)
1/4 cup	white wine (60ml)
1 dash	Tabasco sauce

This recipe comes from the "Settlement Inn," an old stagecoach station north of San Antonio whose specialties are barbecue dishes. The shrimp are marinated, wrapped in bacon, and served grilled as an appetizer.

Preparation

■ Melt the butter in a pot at low heat. Cook the finely diced onions in it for 5 minutes until transparent. Add the ketchup, Worcestershire sauce, steak sauce, vinegar, sugar, water, Tabasco, and wine. Bring to a boil, reduce the heat, and let simmer for 30 minutes in an open pot. Set aside the sauce to cool down.

■ Marinate the shrimp for 30 minutes in the cooled-down sauce. In the meantime, pre-heat the grill.

■ Remove the shrimp from the sauce and individually wrap with a slice of bacon. Cut off the overlaying pieces and use for the smaller shrimp.

■ Stick the shrimp on the skewers. With metal skewers, make sure that they have flattened sides so that the grill meat moves along with them when turning the skewers. Wooden skewers must be soaked for at least one hour so that they do not burn. Round skewers hold the shrimp better whenever 2 little wooden skewers are used.

■ At medium heat grill each side for approximately 3 minutes until the bacon is crispy.

■ Heat the remaining marinade once more and serve as a sauce.

Tipp

As mentioned before, sealable plastic bags are extremely practical for marinating. They very easily open and close with the help of a slider, and in contrast to bowls you save a large amount of marinade because the grill food (here the shrimp) are completely enclosed by the marinade and can be stored airtight.

Salmon Fillet on a Beech Plank

Ingredients (serves 5-10)

Vinaigrette

2 tbsp.	lime juice
2 tbsp.	white balsamic vinegar
2 tbsp.	Dijon mustard
2 tbsp.	honey
2 tbsp.	chives, chopped
1 tsp.	salt
1/2 tsp.	garlic, granulated
1/2 tsp.	black pepper
1/4 tsp.	cayenne pepper
1/4 cup (60ml)	olive oil

Salmon

1	salmon fillet with skin, approximately 3 lbs. (1.5kg)
1	beech plank, untreated, approximately 3/4" (2cm) thick, soaked for at least 2 hours pepper salt

Tagliatelle with Leek Sauce

3-1/2 oz. (100g)	pasta per serving
2 tbsp.	butter
2	shallots
1	garlic clove
1 cup	dry white wine
	salmon remnants
1 bunch	chives, diced
1-2/3 cups (400ml)	cream
	nutmeg
	pepper
	salt

Preparation

■ For the vinaigrette, thoroughly mix all ingredients except for the oil with a hand blender. Emulsify the oil in the mixing process.

■ Trim the salmon and set aside the belly meat. Cut to the skin in portions and season with salt and pepper.

■ Distribute the vinaigrette on the flesh side and also into the cuts.

■ Put the beech plank on the grill for approximately 5 minutes over direct, high heat until smoking and then switch to high, indirect heat so that the plank does not burn.

■ Place the entire salmon fillet on to the plank and grill for 20 to 25 minutes.

■ Cook the pasta according to package directions.

■ Finely chop the shallots and garlic and cook in the butter until transparent. Add the wine and almost completely reduce.

■ Pour the cream on top and reduce to 1/3.

■ Finely dice the salmon remnants and marinate with the diced chives for 2 minutes in the hot sauce and season with salt, pepper, and nutmeg.

■ Mix the sauce and pasta and serve the salmon on top in portions.

Ingredients (serves 4)

4	trout, 1/2 lb. (250g) each
	salt
	pepper
4 sprigs	rosemary
1 tbsp.	butter

Sauce

3 tbsp.	olive oil
1	onion
1	carrot
1 cup	wine
1 can	tomatoes
1/2 tsp.	salt
	pepper
1 tsp.	chili powder
1 tbsp.	parsley, chopped
1 tbsp.	tomato paste

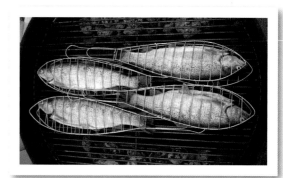

Tip

Inquire about where you can get fresh trout in your area, as there may be a breeding facility where you can purchase freshly caught trout at a good price.

Preparation

■ Dry the gutted fish and season with some salt and pepper. Melt the butter and coat the fish inside and out. Place one sprig of rosemary in each trout **(1)**.

■ For the sauce, heat the oil and lightly sauté the very finely diced onion and finely chopped carrot cubes and add the wine.

■ Pour the juice from the tomato can into a pot and dice the tomatoes. Season with salt, pepper, chili powder, tomato paste, and the chopped parsley. Let the sauce simmer for 20 minutes **(2)**.

■ Place the prepared trout into the oiled fish baskets with the open side inward. Indirectly grill for 15 minutes with a closed lid and serve with the tomato sauce **(3)**.

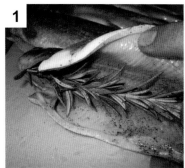

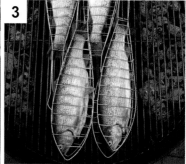

Trout in a lemon butter sauce

Ingredients (serves 3)

3	whole trout
	salt
	pepper
3 sprigs	rosemary
1 tbsp.	basil (as fresh as possible)
1 tbsp.	parsley (as fresh as possible)

Marinade

	juice from a lemon
3 tbsp.	mustard
1 tbsp.	parsley, finely chopped
1 tbsp.	olive oil

Preparation

■ Wash the trout, pat dry, and lightly season with salt and pepper on the inside. Place a bouquet garni with basil, rosemary, and parsley into the cavity (1).

■ Combine mustard, parsley, olive oil, and lemon juice and spread the marinade on the outside of the trout (2).

■ Place the trout in an oiled fish basket and grill with indirect heat for 12 to 15 minutes depending on the size until crispy. Possibly expose to direct heat for a few seconds so that they become crispier (3).

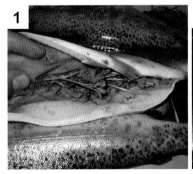

Ingredients (serves 4)

4	John Dory fillets
2	shallots
1 tbsp.	butter
1	zucchini
1	carrot
	white balsamic vinegar
1	tomato
1/4 cup (50ml)	dry white wine
	olive oil
	walnuts, chopped

Preparation

■ Finely dice the shallots and julienne the carrot and zucchini. Seed the tomato and finely dice.

■ Lightly sauté the shallots in butter, add the wine, and, with some white balsamic vinegar, almost completely reduce.

■ Per portion place several vegetable juliennes and diced tomatoes on the center of a 16" x 16" (40x40cm) large square of parchment paper and sprinkle with olive oil (1).

■ Place the fish on top and coat each with 1 tablespoon of shallot sauce, season with salt and pepper, and sprinkle with chopped walnuts (2).

■ Fold the paper into a packet from and tie the ends with string (3).

■ Cook with indirect heat and at approximately 390°F (200°C) for 10 minutes.

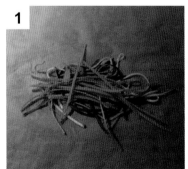

1

2

3

Ingredients (serves 4)

4	jumbo shrimp, small lobsters, or crawfish
	juice from 2 limes
1 tbsp.	fresh thyme, chopped
4	garlic cloves, minced
1/2 tsp.	black pepper

Salsa

l	ripe mango, diced
1/2	large or 1 small red onion, diced
1/2	jalapeño, finely diced
1/2	cucumber, peeled, seeded, and diced
2 tbsp.	coriander leaves, chopped
2 tbsp.	lime juice
	salt
	pepper

Preparation

■ Halve the shrimp with head and shell lengthwise, devein, wash, and blot dry with a paper towel.

■ Mix the lime juice, except for 2 tablespoons, with thyme, garlic, and pepper.

■ Generously brush the shrimp with it on the flesh side and marinate in the refrigerator for 1 hour.

■ For the salsa, prepare all the ingredients, put into a bowl, and mix. Season with salt and pepper.

■ First grill the shrimp at medium, direct heat for 3 minutes on the flesh side, and then turn and finish grilling for 3 more minutes on the shell side.

■ Serve with the mango salsa.

Tipp

With the salsa you can experiment on a whim. Little pieces of tomatoes or red peppers are also suitable. So that it doesn't become too hot you can make the salsa milder with some avocado or before adding the jalapeño remove the skin and seeds.

Ingredients (serves 4)

1 lb. (500g)	green asparagus
1/2 cup (100ml)	white wine
2 pinches	salt
	black pepper
1 pinch	sugar
	butter clumps
	olive oil
1 handful	onions
3	garlic cloves
10	eggs, medium-sized
3 sprigs	fresh dill
1/2 lb. (250g)	smoked salmon
1/2 bunch	arugula

Preparation

■ Peel the asparagus (only the bottom half) and layer into a fitting baking dish. Add the white wine, a pinch of salt and sugar, and clumps of butter **(1)**.

■ Seal the baking dish with aluminum foil and pre-cook in the wood-fired oven at (180°C) for five minutes. The asparagus should still be firm to the bite **(2)**.

■ Halve the asparagus stems crosswise. The halves with the tips are used for decoration. Spread the other half on a well-oiled pizza baking dish **(3)**.

■ Finely chop the onions and garlic, and lightly sauté with a shot of olive oil in a pan until transparent **(4)**.

■ Whip the eggs with a whisk and mix in the onions and garlic. Thoroughly season with black pepper, but add only a pinch of salt **(5)**.

■ Pluck the dill and wash and shake dry the arugula. Cut the smoked salmon into fine strips and mix the arugula and dill with the eggs. Pour the mixture over the asparagus and evenly spread on the pizza baking dish **(6, 7, 8)**.

■ Pre-heat the wood-fired oven to 360-375°F (180-190°C) and then put the dish into the oven and bake for 10 minutes. Now, turn the dish 180 degrees and bake for an additional 10 minutes. The frittata should be just done without the egg becoming dry **(9)**.

■ A fresh salad goes well with this dish.

Ingredients (serves 4)

4   brook trout
     salt
     pepper
1   lemon (according to preference)
     neutral cooking oil or sunflower oil

Preparation

■ Oil the fish basket so that the fish doesn't stick to it during grilling.

■ Brook trout have very fine, flavorful flesh. Therefore, use seasonings sparingly during preparation. Only lightly season the char with salt and pepper and cook on the grill with indirect heat at a maximum of 10 minutes.

■ As soon as the eyes are white, the fish is done.

■ Possibly serve with some lemon juice.

Ingredients (serves 4)

4	tuna steaks, approximately 3/4" to 1" thick (2-3cm)
1/2 cup	honey
1/4 cup	light soy sauce
1/2 tsp.	wasabi powder
1-2/3 cups (300g)	Thai rice
1 small container	saffron
2 tbsp.	peanut oil
	sesame oil
1/2 cup (100ml)	light soy sauce
7 tbsp. (100g)	sesame seed
1	red pepper
1	yellow pepper
6	mushrooms
2	onions, finely diced
	celery
	scallions
	soybean sprouts

Preparation

■ Evenly mix the honey, soy sauce, and wasabi powder (green horseradish). Brush the tuna with the sauce and marinate in the refrigerator for half an hour.

■ Cook the Thai rice with saffron.

■ Fry the rice in a wok with peanut oil, a dash of sesame oil, and some light soy sauce. Wash the peppers, mushrooms, onions, celery, and scallions and cut into small strips. With soybean sprouts, add to the rice in the wok and steam at moderate heat for 10 minutes.

■ Take the tuna from the marinade, pat dry, and coat with sesame seeds on both sides.

■ Grill for 3 minutes on each side covered and at full heat.

■ Serve with the fried rice.

Ingredients (serves 5)

5	pollock fillets

Marinade/Sauce _____

1	garlic clove
1 tsp.	black pepper
2	bay leaves
1 oz.	white wine, dry
1	rosemary sprig
1	thyme sprig
2/3 cup (150g)	crème fraîche
2 tbsp.	olive oil
1/2 cup	fish stock or meat broth
2 tbsp.	onions
	juice from a lemon
8 oz.	container of cream

Preparation

■ Wash the pollock fillet, blot dry, and place into a large bowl.

■ Peel the garlic and crush. Put the ground pepper, bay leaves, white wine with rosemary, thyme, crème fraîche, olive oil, stock, and finely diced onions in a bowl and mix.

■ Marinate the fish fillets for at least 2 to 3 hours (see page 144).

■ Remove the fillets from the marinade and place each in an oiled fish basket. Grill at medium heat on each side for 3 to 5 minutes.

■ For the sauce, strain the marinade to filter out all coarse parts. Add the juice from an entire lemon and a cup of cream, briefly boil, and, at medium heat, reduce to at least half.

Octopus

Ingredients (serves 4)

5	octopus
2 cups	red wine
2	onions
2	garlic cloves
2 tbsp.	sheep milk's cheese seasoning
	olive oil
1	cork

Preparation

■ Wash the octopus in freshwater (if it is frozen, thaw in freshwater).

■ Pour approximately 3 quarts/liters of water into a pot (enough so that the octopus arms can freely move). Add the red wine, 1 diced onion, and the cork and with constant stirring slowly heat to a temperature of 195-200°F (90-94°C) **(1)**. (Do not bring to a boil!)

■ Let the octopus cool down and thoroughly rub with pepper, onion, parsley, fresh garlic, sheep milk's cheese seasoning, and olive oil.

■ In the meantime, pre-heat the wood-fired oven to 390°F (200°C) and then reduce to 320°F (160°C).

■ Cook the octopus in a baking dish for 10 minutes in the wood-fired oven.

> *Tip*
>
> *The wax from the cork settles between the individual protein molecules and prevents an entanglement of the protein. Thus, you achieve a very tender meat texture, which is a rarity with this type of meat.*

1

Ingredients (serves 4)

4	red mullet fillets
4	slices zucchini
4	jumbo shrimp
	pepper
	salt

Marinade

2	garlic cloves
1	large shallot
1/2" (1.5cm)	ginger, peeled
1/2 cup	parsley
1/2 cup	basil
6 tbsp.	olive oil
1 tsp.	lime zest
2 tbsp.	lime juice
1-1/2 tsp.	salt
1 tsp.	paprika
1/2 tsp.	cumin
1/4 tsp.	black pepper

Salad

2 bunch	arugula
2 tbsp.	pine nuts
16	mini tomatoes
4 tbsp.	diced bacon
2	scallions

Vinaigrette

1 tbsp.	Dijon mustard
1 tbsp.	balsamic vinegar
1 tbsp.	honey
2 tbsp.	pumpkin seed oil

Preparation

■ For the marinade, combine all ingredients and chop with a mixer.

■ Cut the zucchini lengthwise in approximately 3/8" (1cm) thick slices.

■ Cover the fish, zucchini slices, and shrimp with the marinade and marinate in the refrigerator for at least two hours (see page 144).

■ Wash the arugula and shake dry. Roast the pine nuts in a pan, cut the tomatoes into quarters, and render the diced bacon in a second pan. Combine all salad ingredients in a large bowl.

■ Make a vinaigrette from mustard, balsamic vinegar, honey, and oil.

■ Place each fish fillet with the skin side up onto a zucchini slice, season with salt and pepper, sprinkle with some oil, and indirectly grill for 12 to 15 minutes at 390°F (200°C).

■ Trim the shrimp and fry in a pan.

■ Arrange the salad in a ring and sprinkle with some vinaigrette. Place a zucchini slice with fish fillet in each center and garnish with a shrimp.

Poultry

Beer Butt **Chicken**

Ingredients (serves 4)

1	chicken
1	beer can, alternatively a baby food jar or a sausages jar
	beer

Brine

10 tbsp.	salt
2 tbsp.	brown sugar
3	bay leaves
3	garlic cloves
1 tsp.	thyme
1 tbsp.	oregano
1	large onion
1 tbsp.	honey
3 tbsp.	soy sauce
2 tbsp.	pepper, white ground
1	lemon
2 cups	orange juice
2 cups	water

Dry rub

1 tsp.	black peppercorn, freshly ground
1 tsp.	celery seed or celery salt
1 tsp.	cayenne pepper
1 tsp.	thyme, dried
1 tsp.	marjoram, dried
2 tsp.	paprika, sweet
1 tbsp.	mustard powder
1 tsp.	salt
1 tbsp.	brown sugar
1	onion, finely grated
4 tbsp.	oil
2 tbsp.	wine vinegar
4 tbsp.	orange juice
4 tbsp.	ketchup
1 tbsp.	Worcestershire sauce
1 dash	Tabasco
1/4 tbsp.	oregano, crushed
1	rosemary sprig

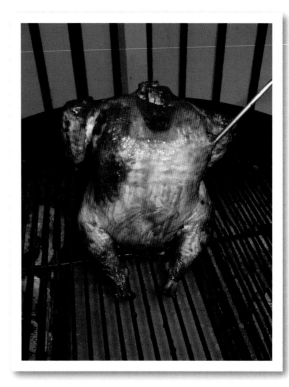

Brine:

A method that increases the liquid content in the meat through osmotic effect and at the same time makes the meat more tender and juicier. You can also thereby season the meat.

Dry rub:

Dry marinade that is massaged into the meat. Alternatively you can brush the chicken with a sweet-sour marinade after half of the cooking time.

Preparation

- Mix the brine and put the chicken in it for 24 hours (1).

- Pat dry the next day and rub with the dry rub.

- Fill the beer can or the other containers two-thirds with beer and sit the chicken on top of the can (2).

- Indirectly cook in a closed kettle grill for approximately 45 to 60 minutes.

- Stick the temperature probe into the breast and set the core temperature to 160°F (72°C).

- From the brine and evaporating beer the chicken will become tender and juicy.

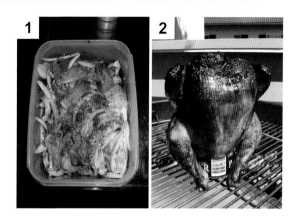

Tipsy **Beer Can Chicken**

Ingredients (serves 8)

2	whole chickens, 2-1/2 lbs. (1.2kg)
1/2 cup (120ml)	olive oil
4	garlic cloves
4	rosemary twigs
3/4 cup (200ml)	beer

Dry Rub ———

3 tbsp. (20g)	ground mustard seed
1 cup (50g)	dried, roasted onions
7 tbsp. (50g)	paprika powder
1 tbsp. (20g)	salt
2 tbsp. (20g)	finely minced garlic
3 tbsp. (20g)	ground coriander
3 tbsp. (20g)	cumin
3 tbsp. (20g)	black pepper, freshly ground

Preparation

- Mix the ingredients for the rub in a bowl.

- First oil the chicken. Now rub the chicken with the dry rub inside and out. Fill the beer into the tray of the poultry holder and set the chicken on the poultry holder.

- Press the garlic by hand and with the rosemary place into the large ring.

- Indirectly cook at medium heat for 1 hour on a charcoal or gas grill.

Ingredients (serves 4)

Seasoning mixture _____

2 tbsp.	yellow curry powder
2 tsp.	salt
2 tsp.	finely minced garlic
2 tsp.	chili flakes
2 tsp.	turmeric
1 tsp.	freshly ground pepper
	coconut milk

Other ingredients _____

1	whole chicken, approximately 2-1/2 lbs. (1.2kg)
1-1/4 cups	beer
1	star anise
1	cinnamon stick

Preparation

■ For the seasoning mixture, combine all ingredients except for the coconut milk and then stir with the coconut milk until a spreadable mixture forms.

■ Wash the chicken and blot dry with paper towels.

■ Put the beer in the inner tray of the chicken holder.

■ Press the star anise and cinnamon stick and place into the drip pan.

■ Brush the chicken with the seasoning mixture on the inside and outside. Seal the neck opening with a cork or with the neck skin and a needle, and bind the wings on the back. Sit on the holder and place in the grill.

■ Indirectly grill for 1 to 1-1/2 hours at approximately 430°F (220°C).

Ingredients (serves 4)

1	chicken, approximately 2-1/2 lbs. (1.2kg)
1 quart	buttermilk
	juice from a lime
2	medium-sized onions
3	scallions
4	garlic cloves
2 tbsp.	fresh oregano
1 tbsp.	fresh thyme
1	rosemary sprig
2	medium chili peppers
2-1/2 tbsp.	salt
3 tbsp.	soy sauce
1 tbsp.	coarse black pepper

Preparation

■ Coarsely chop all ingredients and mix.

■ Stick a portion of the onions, garlic, and herbs into the chicken.

■ Place everything into a plastic bag and marinate for 24 to 48 hours.

■ After marinating, season the chicken with salt and pepper on the inside and outside and possibly add some ground coriander.

■ Fasten the chicken on a rotisserie or sit on a chicken holder and grill for 1 to 1-1/2 hours.

Tip
You can use a different seasoning blend or mix some chili powder with paprika and oil and brush the chicken with it.

Ingredients (serves 4)

2 lbs. (1kg)	chicken wings

Marinade

1 quart	orange juice
2 tbsp.	soy sauce
4 tbsp.	brown sugar
3 tbsp. (60g)	salt
4	garlic cloves
1 tsp.	Tabasco, green
1	chili pepper, diced
4 tbsp.	olive oil

Preparation

■ Combine all ingredients and let the marinade cook for 5 minutes.

■ Preferably marinate the chicken wings overnight in the cooled liquid (however, at least 5 hours).

■ Indirectly grill in a kettle grill for approximately 45 to 60 minutes.

Ingredients (serves 4)

4-1/2 lbs. (2kg)	chicken wings
4 tbsp.	Admins spice blend
4 tbsp.	Hot Elli seasoning salt
1	hot BBQ sauce (i.e., Jim Beam Hot Wings Sauce)

Preparation

■ Rub the wings well with the seasoning blends and marinate in the refrigerator for at least 12 hours.

■ Heat the smoker to 230°F (110°C) and place the chicken wings inside.

■ Mop with the sauce for the first time after 3 hours, repeat this process every 30 minutes.

■ After 4-1/2 hours at 230°F (110°C) the chicken wings are done.

■ White bread and a glass of milk go well with this because the chicken wings are really "HOT."

Curry **Fruit Skewer**

Ingredients (serves 4)

1 lb. (500g)	chicken breast (or already without bones)
2	large slices of pineapple (from a can)
1 can	coconut milk
2	bananas
5	apricots (fresh or dried)
3 tbsp.	oil
3 tbsp.	pineapple juice
2 tbsp.	soy sauce
3 tsp.	curry paste or powder
1 tbsp.	honey
1 tsp.	ginger

Preparation

■ Pour the coconut milk and the curry paste into a bowl. If you do not have curry paste available, curry powder is also suitable. Add the soy sauce and ginger and stir. Pour the marinade into a bag **(1).**

■ If you have already purchased chicken fillet without the bone, then you can skip the next step since the fillet is detached from the breast. In principle, it is very easy; you only need the right tool. An all-purpose tool in the kitchen is a sharp boning knife. With it, you can simply and quickly cut up any pieces of meat into individual portions. The skin is easily pulled from the chicken breast so that both fillet pieces are free. Starting from the breastbone, cut along the bone and pull away the fillet piece somewhat from the center. You will see that it goes quite quickly and hardly any meat remains on the bone. Prepare the second fillet in the same manner.

■ Now, cut the fillet into cubes and place in the marinade. Marinate overnight in the refrigerator. The marinating time can be shortened, but the chicken fillet will not absorb as much flavor.

■ Cut the pineapple and peeled bananas into bite-sized pieces. Cut the fresh apricots into quarters and stone.

■ Stir the heated honey and pineapple juice into a sauce. Skewer the meat and fruit in turns. Grill for 5 minutes and coat once more with the sauce **(2).**

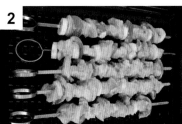

Duck Breast with
citrus-flavored sauce and corn froth

Ingredients (serves 4)

Kumquat ragout

1/4 lb. (100g)	kumquats
2 tbsp.	sugar
1-1/4 cup (300ml)	orange juice
1 tbsp.	bitter orange marmalade
1 tbsp.	sweet marmalade
1 tsp.	starch
3 tbsp.	orange liquor

Corn froth

1 tbsp.	sugar
1/4 lb. (100g)	sweet corn
2 tbsp.	butter
1/4 cup (50ml)	white port wine
1/2 cup (100ml)	cream
	salt
	cayenne pepper

Duck breast

1-2	duck breast fillets with skin
	five-spice powder
	salt and pepper
	oil

Preparation

■ Prick the kumquats multiple times with a needle and blanch two times, three minutes each in fresh water. Slightly caramelize the sugar, add the orange juice, and reduce for 10 minutes.

■ In the meantime, divide the kumquats into quarters and seed. Put the kumquat wedges in the orange juice and boil down once again for 5 minutes. Dissolve the starch in a little bit of water and slightly bind the mixture. Stir in the marmalades and orange liquor. Keep everything warm.

■ For the corn froth, lightly brown the sugar. Add the corn kernels, butter, and port wine and stir in the cream. Let everything lightly simmer for 10 minutes and season with salt and cayenne pepper.

■ Purée to the desired consistency with cream at low heat and beat until slightly frothy. Keep warm.

■ Trim the duck breast, make diamond-shaped cuts on the skin, season with salt, pepper, and five-spice powder. Lightly oil. Grill on a griddle in the grill on the skin side for 5 minutes at 390-450°F (200-230°C). Turn over once and grill for 5 minutes on the flesh side.

■ Let rest for 5 minutes in aluminum foil, cut into even slices, and serve with ragout and corn froth. Sprinkle some sea salt and coarse black pepper on the slices.

Ingredients (serves 4)

1	chicken
	juice from 4 oranges
	juice from a lime
2 cups (500ml)	unfiltered apple juice
1/2 cup (200ml)	beer
2	medium-sized onions
3	scallions
4	garlic cloves
10 slices	fresh ginger
2 tbsp.	fresh oregano
1 tbsp.	fresh thyme
2	medium chili peppers (here 1 red and 1 yellow)
2-1/2 tbsp.	salt
3 tbsp.	soy sauce
1 tbsp.	white pepper
1 tbsp.	coarse black pepper
1 tsp.	cinnamon
1 tbsp.	honey
2-1/2 tbsp.	cane sugar

Preparation

■ Coarsely chop everything that you can cut and mix together all ingredients. Place a portion of the onions and garlic with the herbs into the chicken.

■ Store the chicken in a closed container or shrink-wrapped in a cool place for 24 hours. During this time, the meat absorbs the flavors of the ingredients and becomes wonderfully tender and juicy.

You will find more information on the topic of brining on page 58.

Poultry Skewers with Sweet-and-Sour and Curry Marinades

Ingredients (serves 4)

3 pieces   chicken fillet
3 pieces   turkey fillet
3   onions

Sweet-and-Sour Marinade _____

10 tbsp.   ketchup
2 tbsp.   white balsamic vinegar
2 tbsp.   Worcestershire sauce
1 tsp.   chili powder
1 bunch   rosemary
1 tbsp.   maple syrup
2 tbsp.   honey
1 tbsp.   paprika
           salt and pepper

Curry Marinade _____

3 tbsp.   curry powder or preferably curry paste
1/2 tsp.   cinnamon
1 tsp.   ginger
           cream, until the marinade becomes quite fluid (approximately 5 tbsp.)

Preparation

■ Mix the ingredients for both marinades. Cut the poultry into cubes and marinate overnight — place the chicken fillets in the sweet-and-sour marinade and the turkey fillets in the curry marinade.

1

■ Cut up the onions; for each 2 skewers, use one onion. Alternate between chicken/onion/turkey until the skewer is full. If you use 2 skewers, the grill food can be more easily turned on the grate (1).

■ Briefly directly grill and indirectly cook for a few minutes. Alternately, directly grill at medium heat.

Ingredients (serves 2)

Quails

2	quails
1/4 lb. (100g) ea.	mixed ground meat and ground pork
1 tbsp.	flaked almonds
2 oz. (50g)	dried mixed fruit
1 tbsp.	raisins
1	egg yolk
2 pinches ea.	ground pepper, cloves, nutmeg, and ginger
	rosemary and thyme sprigs
	salt and pepper
	oil
	butter

Leeks

2 stems	leek
1 tbsp.	pine nuts
1 tbsp.	raisins
1 cup (250ml)	cream
	salt, pepper, and sugar
	dry Riesling

Preparation

■ Roast the almonds and coarsely cut the mixed fruit.

■ Combine the mixed ground meat, ground pork, fruit, almonds, raisins, and egg yolk and season with salt, pepper, and mixture of ground pepper, cloves, nutmeg and ginger.

■ Fill the quails with the mixture and season on the outside with salt and pepper. Sear the quails in oil with rosemary and thyme in a cast iron pan and then finish indirectly grilling for approximately 30 minutes at 390°F (200°C). Raise the heat for the last 10 minutes so that the skin becomes nicely brown and crispy while brushing with liquid butter.

■ For the leeks, clean the leek stems and cut into juliennes. Season with salt, pepper, and sugar.

■ Sauté the pine nuts and raisins in oil, add the leeks, and cook together for 5 minutes.

■ Add wine to the vegetables, add the cream, and cook until firm to the bite.

■ Season with nutmeg, salt, and pepper and finish cooking.

Ingredients (serves 4)

1	chicken
2	limes, their juice
2 tbsp.	brown sugar
	pepper
	white wine

Sauce

1 can	peeled tomatoes, coarsely diced
1 tbsp.	white wine vinegar
2	shallots, finely diced
1	garlic clove, crushed
1/4 tsp.	salt
1/4 tsp.	pepper
1/2 tsp.	coriander
2	limes, their juice
	olive oil (1 double shot glass)
	white wine (1 double shot glass)

Preparation

■ Mix all ingredients for the sauce and pour into a plastic bag. Place the chicken in the bag and marinate overnight. Carefully shake well several times to evenly distribute the marinade.

■ The next day fill white wine in the chicken holder or in a sausages jar and set the chicken on top. Brush with the lime juice and place onto the grill grate **(1)**.

■ Cook with indirect heat and a closed lid for approximately 45 minutes until a core temperature of 160°F (72°C) has been reached. Occasionally coat with lime juice.

■ Meanwhile, add the brown sugar to the sauce and thicken for at least 20 minutes **(2)**.

■ Carve the chicken with poultry scissors and serve with the sauce.

■ Rice goes especially well with this dish.

Ingredients (serves 4-6)

1-3/4 lbs. (800g)	medium-sized onions
6	chili peppers
3-1/2 oz. (100g)	black olives
3	cinnamon sticks
12	bay leaves
1-3/4 cups (400ml)	poultry stock
1-3/4 cups (400ml)	marsala semi seco (Italian wine)
1/2 cup (100 ml)	orange juice
3-1/2 oz. (100g)	honey
3-1/2 oz. (100g)	roasted pine nuts
7 oz. (200g)	prunes
1 bunch	parsley
8	chicken legs, approximately 5-1/2 lbs. (2.5kg)
	roast chicken seasoning

Preparation

■ Peel and cut the onions into quarters, but do not remove the root end (you don't want them to fall apart). Quarter the chili peppers lengthwise and set the stalk and seeds to the side.

■ Choose a sufficiently large baking dish and spread everything together with the olives, cinnamon sticks, and bay leaves in it **(1)**.

■ Mix together the poultry stock, marsala semi seco (wine), orange juice, and honey and pour over the ingredients in the baking dish. The onions should slightly protrude from the stock **(2)**.

■ Remove the excess fat from the chicken legs; at the joint, the skin and tendon are severed and the joint taken off **(3)**.

■ Massage the legs with some olive oil and powder with roast chicken seasoning **(4)**.

■ Loosely cover with aluminum foil **(5)**.

■ Heat the wood-fired oven to approximately 430°F (220°C) and insert the baking dish for 1 hour **(6, 7)**.

■ Remove the aluminum foil and pour the broth over the legs. Add the prunes and plucked parsley **(8)**.

■ Insert baking dish without foil into the oven for an additional 15 minutes and then pour on top once more and let simmer in the oven for 15 minutes **(9)**.

■ Place a leg, the skimmed onions, and olives on a plate and sprinkle with the roasted pine nuts.

■ Rice goes especially well with this.

1

2

3

4

5

6

7

8

9

Ingredients (serves 4)

1	turkey thigh, without bones
3	sun-dried tomatoes
4 stalks	scallions
3 tbsp.	Admins grill seasoning
2 tbsp.	Hot Elli seasoning salt
	salt
	pepper
5	habaneros
2	grilled bell peppers
2	shallots
3	garlic cloves
5	tomatoes

Preparation

■ Cut the thigh flat and season with the seasoning blends, salt, and pepper inside and out. Wrap the sun-dried tomatoes and scallions in the thigh. Tie up with butcher's string **(1)**.

■ Grill the peppers until the skin is black and then remove the skin. Seed the habaneros and put in a mixer with the garlic and skinned peppers and stir into a smooth mixture. Rub the turkey roll completely with it **(2)**.

■ Heat the smoker to 250°F (120°C) and place the turkey roll inside.

■ Make the mop sauce from some sunflower oil or olive oil and seasoning blends. Skin the tomatoes and chop with an immersion blender. Season with salt and pepper.

■ The turkey is mopped for the first time after two hours — this process should be repeated every 30 minutes.

■ The temperature should not exceed 250°F (120°C).

■ The entire cooking time amounts to 4-1/2 hours. The turkey should have a core temperature of 170°F (75°C) **(3)**.

1

2

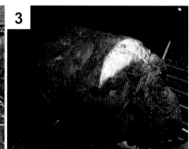
3

Ingredients (serves 4)

1/4 lb. (100g)	iceberg lettuce
1	tomato
1	cucumber
1	chili pepper
1	mango
1/4 cup (50g)	crème fraîche
	salt and pepper
4	tortillas
3 oz. (80g)	grated Emmentaler cheese
7 oz. (200g)	chicken breast
5 oz. (150g)	pork fillet

Marinades

1	lime
1	chili pepper
1 sprig	fresh rosemary
2	garlic cloves
1/4 cup (50ml)	olive oil
1/2 cup (100g)	ajvar (relish)
2 sprigs	mint
2	garlic cloves
1/4 cup (50ml)	coconut milk

Tip
So that the meats can marinate well, it is recommended to begin marinating the day prior.

Preparation

■ Grate the lime peel, cut the chili peppers with seeds into fine, small rings, and pluck the rosemary sprig against the grain. Peel the garlic and cut into fine slices.

■ Put all ingredients into a bowl. Add the olive oil and lime juice and marinate the chicken breast in it. Stir the coconut milk with the ajvar (relish) until smooth, peel the garlic, and mince together with the mint.

■ Put all ingredients into a bowl and marinate the pork fillet in them.

■ The following day, remove both bowls from the refrigerator 1 hour before grilling.

■ Cut the iceberg lettuce into fine strips and cut the tomatoes, cucumber, and mango into 3/8" (1cm) large cubes.

■ Directly grill the marinated meat at high heat.

■ Spread one side of the tortillas with crème fraîche. Cut the grilled meat into 3/8" thick (1cm) slices and spread together with the vegetables and fruit onto a half of the tortilla. Sprinkle cheese on top.

■ Now fold the quesadillas in half, coat both sides with oil, and place on the grill briefly until the cheese melts.

Ingredients (serves 4-6)

3	chicken breast fillets
2	ripe tomatoes, seeded and skinned
1	green pepper
1	red pepper
1	medium-sized onion
2	garlic cloves
1	Thai chili pepper
3 tbsp.	diced bacon
1/4 lb. (100g)	mild gouda
1/4 lb. (100g)	cheddar, Gruyère, or Bergkäse
6	wheat tortillas (tacos, fajitas, wraps, or taboon bread)
8 oz. (227g)	crème fraîche

Preparation

■ Quarter the red and green peppers, remove the seeds, stem, and ribs and lightly oil. Grill over direct heat until the skin bubbles and the peppers are black. Let cool, pull off the skin, remove the black spots, and with the tomatoes cut into cubes.

■ Lightly oil the chicken breast fillets and grill over direct heat for 4 minutes, turning once. Let cool and cut into 3/8" thick (1cm) slices.

■ Finely dice the onion, garlic, and chili pepper. For less hotness, you can remove the seeds of the chili pepper beforehand.

■ Render the diced bacon in a pan until crispy and let cool on a paper towel.

■ Grate the cheese.

■ Spread some crème fraîche on a wrap. On one half add some tomato-pepper mixture and sprinkle with diced bacon.

■ Place the chicken slices on top, season with salt and pepper, and spread with the onion mixture. Cover everything with cheese. Fold together in the center (see below) and lightly press.

■ Grill at 390°F (200°C) for 2 to 3 minutes on each side until the cheese has melted.

  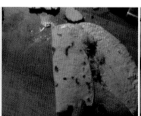 

Ingredients

3 cups (700ml)	water, lukewarm
4 tsp.	salt
1/2 cube	yeast
2 lbs. (1kg)	wheat flour, type 550

Preparation

■ Dissolve the salt and yeast in the water, and then add all of the flour and knead for 2 minutes.

■ Transfer the dough into a large and lightly oiled bowl. Let rise for 2 hours at room temperature and then place in the refrigerator for 24 hours.

■ The next day, remove the dough from the refrigerator and cut in half.

■ On a well-floured surface, form a round loaf. Thoroughly sprinkle the loaf once more with flour and score multiple times.

■ The other half of the dough can be stored in the refrigerator again. It will be good for approximately 10 to 14 days. During this time, the dough still matures and the bread becomes more aromatic.

■ The dough can also be made with other types of flour, for example always 50% wheat flour type 500 and 50% whole grain wheat, wholemeal spelt, or durum wheat flour.

■ Heat the wood-fired oven to 840°F (450°C); maintain this temperature for at least 30 minutes and then clear the heat source from the firebox, close the flue damper, and wipe the firebricks with a wet cloth. Monitor the temperature of the firebricks. Also add some semolina on the stone. It may not burn, but rather only become brown after a few seconds.

■ Place the bread into the oven and immediately spray with a spray bottle filled with water. After 15 minutes, turn the bread 180 degrees and repeat the steaming. After approximately 30 to 40 minutes, you can do the knock test. Using your knuckles, knock on the bottom side of the bread. The bread is done when a "hollow" sound is heard when knocking.

Ingredients (serves 4)

2 packets	dry yeast
4 tsp.	baking powder
3-1/2 cups (800ml)	water, lukewarm
3 lbs. (1400g)	flour
1-1/2 tbsp. (20g)	olive oil
1-1/2 tbsp. (20g)	sugar
1 tbsp. (20g))	coarse salt
7 oz. (200g)	sun-dried tomatoes, diced

Preparation

- Dissolve the yeast in lukewarm water.

- Add the oil, sugar, and salt.

- Sift in the flour and with the tomatoes knead into an elastic dough.

- Divide the dough into 10 even portions and let rise for 15 minutes.

- Pre-heat a pizza stone for 15 minutes.

- Indirectly grill the rolls at 430°F (220°C) for 15 to 20 minutes.

Ingredients (serves 4)

1 head	cabbage
1	carrot
2 tsp.	onions
1/3 cup	sugar
1/2 tsp.	salt
1/2 tsp.	pepper
1/4 cup	milk
1/2 cup	mayonnaise
1/4 cup	buttermilk
2 tbsp.	white wine vinegar
2 tbsp.	lemon juice

Preparation

■ With a food processor, chop the washed cabbage, onion, and carrot into small pieces approximately the size of a grain of rice **(1)**.

■ Place the vegetables in a large bowl and add the sugar, salt, pepper, milk, mayonnaise, buttermilk, vinegar, and lemon juice. Mix well **(2)**.

■ Let marinate covered for at least 2 hours in the refrigerator before serving. The coleslaw tastes even better if you prepare it the night before.

Ingredients (serves 4)

2	red peppers
2	green peppers
2	small zucchinis
2	tomatoes
	salt
	pepper
2	garlic cloves, finely minced
1	medium-sized red onion, finely diced
7 oz (200g)	Bergkäse cheese, grated
8 oz (227g)	crème fraîche
12	wraps, approximately 5 1/8" (13cm)

Preparation

■ Lightly oil the zucchinis and peppers and grill. Let the peppers turn black.

■ Let the peppers cool down covered until the skin has loosened and then remove the skin. Skin and seed the tomatoes.

■ Cut the peppers, zucchinis, and tomatoes into small cubes and place into a colander. Season with salt, pepper, and garlic.

■ If necessary, cut out the wraps at a diameter of approximately 5-1/8" (13cm) **(1)**.

■ Spread crème fraîche on one side of the wraps, spread the vegetable mixture on top, and then the onions and cheese **(2)**.

■ Fold the wraps and fix with a string.

■ Grill at medium heat for 2 to 4 minutes until the edges of the wraps are brown and the cheese has melted.

Vegetables from the Wok

Ingredients (serves 8)

14 oz. (400g)	zucchinis
14 oz. (400g)	fennel bulbs
7 oz. (200g)	red peppers
7 oz. (200g)	yellow peppers
3-1/2 oz. (100g)	red onions
1/2 cup (100ml)	olive oil
3/4 cup (180ml)	vegetable broth
2	garlic cloves, whole, peeled
2	rosemary sprigs
	coarse salt
	pepper

Preparation

■ Cut the zucchini, fennel, and peppers into 3/8" (1cm) wide strips.

■ Cut the onions and garlic in 1/4" (.5cm) size cubes.

■ Pour oil into the hot wok. As soon as there are light streaks in the oil, put the vegetables into the wok and sauté until firm to the bite.

■ After approximately 2 minutes, add the rosemary and season with broth, salt, and pepper.

Tip
This recipe can be varied by using different types of vegetables, such as sugar peas, carrots, or leeks.

Guacamole-Dip

Zutaten (für 4 Personen)

2	ripe avocados
2	tomatoes, seeded and skinned
	juice from 1/2 lime
2	garlic cloves
1 tbsp.	natural yogurt
	salt
	pepper

Preparation

■ Cut the avocado in half and remove the pit. Take out the flesh of the fruit and mash or puree.

■ Skin the tomatoes, seed, and cut into small cubes. Finely mince the garlic cloves.

■ Mix the avocado puree, tomato cubes, garlic, yogurt, and lime juice in a bowl and season with salt and pepper.

■ It tastes good with potato wedges, tortillas, and everything else that you can dip.

Strawberry Salsa

Ingredients (serves 4)

1	cucumber
1	scallion
1 tbsp.	fresh mint
3 tbsp.	rice wine vinegar (white wine vinegar as an alternative)
1/2 lb. (250g)	fresh strawberries, stems removed and finely diced

Preparation

▪ Finely dice the cucumber. Cut the scallion into fine little rolls and the mint into fine strips.

▪ Combine the vegetables with vinegar in a medium-sized bowl. Cover with foil and marinate in the refrigerator for 1 hour.

▪ Remove the stems from the strawberries, finely dice, and mix into the salsa shortly before serving.

Grilled Vegetable Gratin

Ingredients (serves 6)

6-8	firm, ripe tomatoes
2	small zucchinis
1	red pepper
1 tbsp.	fresh basil, chopped
1/2 tsp.	garlic, minced
4	eggs
1/2 cup (100ml)	milk
1 cup	cheese (Gruyère or Bergkäse)
1 cup	soft toast crumbs
1 tbsp.	Parmesan, grated
	olive oil
	pepper
	salt

Preparation

■ Lightly oil the zucchinis and pepper and directly grill at medium heat. The pepper needs approximately 10 minutes, the zucchinis approximately 6 minutes. After half of the time, turn over one time each.

■ Let the vegetables cool down and then remove the pepper skin.

■ Skin and seed the tomatoes.

■ Dice the vegetables and place into a colander.

■ Stir the eggs and milk in a bowl, then mix in the grated cheese, diced vegetable, chopped basil, and minced garlic and season with salt and pepper.

■ Place the mixture into a cast iron pan of approximately 8" to 10" (20-25cm) diameter and sprinkle with bread crumbs and grated Parmesan.

■ Grill over direct, low heat for 20 to 25 minutes until the edges are brown.

Tip
Based on the grill, it is advisable to decouple the pan. This means do not set it directly on the grate, but rather somewhat raised.

Greek Wood-Fired Oven **Pizza**

Ingredients (serves 4)

Dough

1 lb. (500g)	flour
1 packet	dry yeast
1 tsp.	salt
1/2 tsp.	sugar
1 cup	water, lukewarm
1-2 tbsp.	olive oil

Topping

	Pizza sauce
1	chili
1 pack	sheep milk's cheese, Greek or Sardinian
1 tbsp.	fresh thyme, chopped
	pepper
	salt
12 oz. (350g)	ground beef
2-3 tsp.	Greek seasoning blend / herbs
12 oz. (350g)	Emmentaler cheese

Preparation

■ For the dough, put the flour, dry yeast, salt, sugar, lukewarm water, and olive oil into a bowl and mix well (use a food processor if necessary). Let rise in a warm area for approximately 40 minutes.

■ Once again, thoroughly knead the dough by hand. Divide the dough into 4 small, round portions and roll out on a floured surface.

■ For the topping, spread the pizza sauce on the dough base.

■ Chop the sheep milk's cheese and sprinkle with some fresh thyme. Cut the chili into fine rings.

■ Brown the ground beef and season with salt and pepper, and then spread over the tomato sauce and cover with chili, sheep milk's cheese, and grated Emmentaler cheese. Evenly spread the Greek seasoning blend on top.

■ Bake the pizza in a wood-fired oven with increasing heat at 600°F (320°C) for 2 to 4 minutes.

Pizza Marguerita

Ingredients (serves 6)

Dough

2 lbs. (1kg)	fine durum wheat flour
2 cups	water, lukewarm
3 tbsp. (40g)	yeast, fresh
1 tbsp. (15g)	coarse sea salt
1 tsp.	sugar
4 tbsp.	olive oil

Tomato sauce

1 small can	plum tomatoes
	salt
	pepper
1 tbsp.	tomato paste
1 tbsp.	ketchup
1 tbsp.	sugar
1 tsp.	fresh oregano, finely chopped
1 tsp.	onion powder
1 tsp.	balsamic vinegar

Topping

1 small can	plum tomatoes
2 tbsp.	basil, coarsely chopped
	Mozzarella
	Pizza herbs

Preparation

■ Dissolve the yeast in the water with 1 cup (100g) of flour, olive oil, salt, and sugar. Gradually add the remaining flour and knead well. Let rise in a warm area for at least 4 hours. Knead approximately once per hour.

■ Form 7 balls from the dough and let rise again for 1 hour.

■ Heat the grill and position the charcoal baskets in the center at a distance of 3" (7cm). Place the pizza stone on the grate and heat the temperature to the maximum with a closed grill lid.

■ For the tomato sauce, puree the plum tomatoes, mix with the other ingredients, and marinate in the refrigerator for 2 hours.

■ Brush a pizza pan with olive oil and roll out a dough ball on top to form a pizza base. Spread one ladle of sauce on top. Cut the plum tomatoes into extremely thin slices, lightly salt, and spread with basil on the pizza. Cover with very thinly cut, firm mozzarella according to preference.

■ Place the pizza with the pizza pan into a second pizza pan and position in the center of the pizza stone. Bake covered for 10 minutes at the highest temperature.

■ Remove the pizza from the grill, sprinkle lightly with dried pizza herbs, and serve immediately.

Pizza with Parma Ham, Arugula, and Parmesan

Ingredients (serves 4)

Dough

28 oz. (800g)	flour
1-2/3 cups (400ml)	lukewarm water
2 packets	dry yeast
2 tsp.	sugar
4 tsp.	salt
8 tbsp.	olive oil

Topping

7 oz. (200g)	fresh arugula, cleaned
3-1/2 oz. (100g)	Parmesan, broken from one piece or sliced
18 slices	Parma ham or Serrano
1 pack	gratin or pizza cheese, grated
1 packet	chunky peeled tomatoes with herbs or the like

Preparation

■ For the dough, place the flour, yeast, sugar, and salt into a mixing bowl and mix well.

■ Add the water and then the olive oil and knead for approximately 8 minutes. Increase the amount of water as needed until the dough is nicely smooth and no longer sticks to the bowl.

■ Divide the dough into six even portions and let rise covered in a warm area.

■ Knead the pieces of dough once more and on a floured surface roll out to the desired size.

■ Spread the tomato sauce on the rolled out pizza base, sprinkle with some pizza cheese, and place the pizza on the grill.

■ When the cheese is lightly browned, cover each pizza with 3 slices of ham. Continue grilling the pizza for approximately 2 minutes.

■ Cover the pizza with arugula and Parmesan and serve hot.

Tip
You can naturally vary the ingredients, for example, with thin mushrooms or anchovies. To please the eye, you can also garnish the finished pizza with some balsamic reduction.

Ingredients (serves 4)

Dough _____

1 lb. (500g)	flour
1 tsp.	salt
1 packet	fresh yeast
2/3 cup (150ml)	warm water
1/4 cup (50ml)	milk
2 tbsp.	olive oil

Base topping _____

14 oz. (400g)	tomato puree with oregano and basil
7 oz. (200g)	Emmentaler cheese, 45% fat

Toppings according to preference _____

Salami, ham, onions, capers, anchovies, artichokes, pineapple

Preparation

■ For the dough, put the flour, salt, yeast, warm water, and a shot of milk into a mixing bowl and blend with the dough hooks until the dough loosens from the bowl. To get the most workable dough, it should be kneaded for at least 10 minutes. Now, place dough portions of different sizes at a large distance from each other onto a floured base. Let rise, covered with a kitchen towel, for 30 to 45 minutes until the volume has nearly doubled.

■ Oil the cast iron pan. Do not roll out the dough, but rather turn the dough portions in the air until they have reached the correct thickness. It happens completely without force, but with the help of gravity. The pizza base should be thin because it rises during baking. With a spoon, apply the tomato puree and then sprinkle the cheese on top.

■ For the topping, first spread the tomato sauce and cheese onto the pizza base and then cover with toppings according to preference.

■ Cover the charcoal grate of the kettle grill all around with charcoal and spare the center of the grate so that the pizza also gets much heat from above and doesn't burn too quickly on the bottom. Place the pizza pan onto the hot kettle grill. Close the lid and cook for 10 to 15 minutes.

■ Resist the temptation to lift the lid in the meantime. The earliest you may lift it is after 8 minutes; otherwise all of the heat escapes. If the bottom is lightly brown, the pizza is done. You will also recognize it when the pizza bubbles. Take the pizza immediately out of the cast iron pan; otherwise the bottom will become too hard.

Tips

Never sprinkle the cheese on the toppings, but rather on top of the tomato sauce and then put the different toppings on top.

Additional pizzas are easy to prepare. Make sure that they are placed on floured parchment paper and then you can transport them with the help of a board to the grill and slide the pizzas into the pan. Or within a few seconds put the dough on the still-warm pan. With the residual heat, it additionally rises.

Vera Pizza Napoletana

Ingredients (serves 4)

Dough

2-1/3 cups (555ml)	water, lukewarm
2 lbs. (1kg)	flour, type 00
1-1/2 tbsp. (28g)	sea salt
1/2 tsp. (1.7g)	yeast

The ingredients should always be at room temperature.

Topping

6	beefsteak tomatoes
4	mozzarella
	olive oil
	sea salt
	black pepper
	basil
	Basilikum

Preparation

▪ Dissolve the yeast in water and then add salt and dissolve.

▪ First fold in 3/4 cup (100g) of flour. Now, slowly add the remaining flour within 10 minutes with constant stirring. Continue kneading for 20 minutes at the slowest level until a soft, elastic dough forms that does not stick.

▪ Let the dough rise covered for 2 hours in a lightly oiled bowl at room temperature.

▪ Divide the dough into 6 even portions. On a lightly floured table surface, knead the dough pieces in the palm of your hand to form balls. Let the balls rise in a closed container for 6 hours at room temperature.

▪ Score the tomatoes crosswise and dip into boiling water for 10 seconds. Now, rinse with cold water and skin. Remove the stem and seeds and cut the flesh into small cubes.

▪ Let the tomato cubes, together with a dash of olive oil, simmer for 2 to 3 minutes at low heat. The flesh should not become too soft.

▪ Cut the mozzarella into strips.

▪ Heat the wood-fired oven to 660-700°F (350-370°C) and maintain this temperature.

▪ Press the dough balls flat with the palm of your hand and form a flatbread with your fingers; work your fingertips from the inside out until the flatbread has a thickness of approximately 3/16" (4mm). You should do this without the help of a rolling pin because the pressure destroys the fine dough structure.

▪ Spread the tomatoes on the dough, season with sea salt and black pepper, and then put the mozzarella and some basil on top and season with several dashes of olive oil.

▪ Clean the firebrick with a wet cloth. The temperature of the stone can be tested with some semolina (wheat middlings). Sprinkle the wheat on the stone. It should not burn, but rather take on a light brown color after a few seconds. If the stone is too hot, it can be cooled down with water from a spray bottle.

▪ Put the pizza in the oven and bake for 3 to 4 minutes. After 2 minutes, turn 180 degrees.

Tip
Always bake pizza "at sight": for this always monitor the bottom of the pizza.

Potato Salad

Ingredients (serves 4)

1 lb. (500g) potatoes, waxy
2 tbsp. sunflower oil
4 tbsp. wine vinegar
1 can meat broth
1 tbsp. parsley, chopped
　　　　 salt
　　　　 pepper

Preparation

■ Boil the potatoes for approximately 40 minutes, or until they are soft when poked with a fork. Briefly rinse with cold water and peel while warm.

■ Dice a small onion and put into a bowl.

■ Cut the potatoes with an egg slicer in even slices and add with finely chopped parsley to the onions.

■ Pour warm meat broth on top. The potatoes that are still warm absorb the liquid after a few minutes and the taste improves.

■ Add vinegar, salt, and pepper on top, mix, and let marinate for at least 30 minutes.

■ Finally, add the sunflower oil. Note: It is important that the oil is added only at the end; otherwise the potatoes will close and no longer absorb any liquid.

Garlic Baguettes
with Taleggio and Fig Mustard

Ingredients (serves 6)

6	thin slices of baguette
1	garlic clove
1-2	figs
2-1/2 oz. (75g)	Taleggio (Italian soft cheese)
	fig mustard

Preparation

■ Toast the baguette slices on the grill on both sides.

■ Halve the garlic clove and rub the bread on the cut surfaces.

■ Halve the figs and then cut into a total of 6 nice slices and place on the baguette slices (1).

■ Layer 1 slice of Taleggio on each of the figs.

■ Indirectly grill the baguettes until the cheese begins to melt.

■ Place a teaspoon of fig mustard in the center and serve immediately (2).

Ingredients (serves 4)

1 pack	lasagna sheets
	cheese, grated

For the Bolognese sauce

12 oz. (350g)	ground beef
1/2 lb. (250g)	mozzarella
2	onions
2	carrots
1-1/2 tbsp. (2cl)	tomato paste
1 large can	tomatoes
7 oz. (200ml)	red wine
	salt, pepper
	olive oil
1 tsp.	basil
1/2 tsp.	oregano
1 tsp.	rosemary
1-2	garlic cloves (optional)

For the Béchamel sauce

3 tbsp. (40g)	butter
1/3-cup (40g)	flour
1-1/4 cup (300ml)	milk
	nutmeg
	salt

Preparation

■ For the Bolognese sauce, dice the onions and carrots and brown in hot olive oil for 5 minutes. Now, add the ground beef and brown with constant stirring.

■ Pour the red wine on top and briefly simmer.

■ Fill the canned tomatoes into a high container (here a measuring cup of 1 to 1-1/2 quarts/liters is suggested) and with an immersion blender form a smooth mixture. Also add to the pot.

■ Now, add the tomato paste. Here a product that is already seasoned with root vegetables and is measured in a shot glass 1-1/2 tbsp. (2cl) is recommended.

■ Add the spices — depending on the time of year, they should be as fresh as possible from the garden. Naturally, garlic goes well here; cut in 1 to 2 cloves, according to preference.

■ Let the sauce simmer for at least 45 minutes. It has reached the correct consistency when a cooking spoon that is placed in it remains standing for a few seconds.

■ For the Béchamel sauce, melt the butter and mix in the flour with a whisk. Immediately, gradually add milk and continue cooking; the sauce will increasingly thicken. If it becomes too thick, add some milk and continue to stir so that no clumps form. For the lasagna, the consistency should not be too thin, but rather become easily spreadable.

■ Add a thin layer of Bolognese sauce in the oiled oven and cover with lasagna sheets. Fill the gaps with broken off sheets and then add a layer of the Béchamel sauce, a layer of cheese, and lasagna sheets again. Make sure that the lasagna ends with a layer of Béchamel sauce. Combine this with some Bolognese sauce to get a nice color. Finally, sprinkle some cheese on top.

■ After 45 minutes, the lasagna is done.

Tip
Frozen in portions, the sauce provides a quick starting point for baked pasta and quick noodle dishes.

Ingredients (serves 4)

10-1/2 oz. (300g)	pikeperch fillet
	salt
8	basil leaves
12	mangel beet leaves, blanched

Stuffing

12 oz. (350g)	salmon fillet
10 oz. (280g)	cream
2	egg whites
	salt

Sauce

7 oz. (200ml)	fish stock
3 oz. (100ml)	cream
3 oz. (80g)	cold butter, cubed
3-1/2 tbsp. (5cl)	dry white wine

Parsnips puree

1 lb. (500g)	parsnips
4 tbsp	shallots, diced
1-1/2 tbsp. (20g)	butter
3-1/2 tbsp. (5cl)	poultry stock
1 shot	cream
	juice from 1/2 lime
	salt
	pepper

Preparation

■ Cut 4 equally sized pieces from the pikeperch fillet, season with salt, and cover each with two leaves of basil. Dice the very cold salmon fillet, mix with two egg whites, season with salt, and finely puree in a mixer. Strain the salmon mixture and carefully stir with the stiffly whipped cream so that a smooth stuffing forms.

■ Blanch the mangel beet leaves and then remove the hard stem. Place 3 of the leaves each in a soup ladle so that they stand over the edge. Lightly salt, add some salmon stuffing, set a piece of pikeperch fillet with basil on top. Spread on the salmon stuffing again. Seal everything with the overlaying mangel beet.

■ Set the chocolate almond pralines in a pot, pour in the white wine and fish stock, and, with a closed lid, place in the oven pre-heated to 390°F (200°C) for 20 minutes.

■ Peel and dice the parsnips. Lightly sauté with the diced shallots in butter, season with salt and pepper, and cook with poultry stock and a shot of cream for 15 minutes until soft. Puree with a hand blender, then season with lime juice.

■ Now, take the chocolate almond pralines from the pot. Add cream to the wine-fish stock, briefly boil, and with a whisk stir in cold butter cubes.

■ Put the parsnips puree on the center of a plate, place a sliced mangelwurzel praline on top, and pour on sauce.

Mushroom Skewers

Ingredients (serves 12)

24	mushrooms
3 tbsp.	olive oil
3	shallots, finely chopped
6 tbsp.	leek
	pepper
	salt
2 pinches	curry
2/3 cup	cream (150ml)
24 slices	bacon

Preparation

■ Twist the stalks from the mushroom caps and finely dice.

■ Cut the leek into fine rings.

■ Braise the shallots, diced mushrooms, and leek rings in olive oil and season with salt, pepper, and curry. Add the cream and reduce to half.

■ Fill the mushrooms with the mixture and smooth out.

■ With the filling inward place together two mushrooms, each wrapped crosswise with two slices of bacon and skewer lengthwise.

■ Grill at 480°F (250°C) for approximately 5-7 minutes until the bacon has a nice color.

Sauerkraut Pancakes

Ingredients (serves 16)

1 can	sauerkraut, 1/2 pint (285ml) weight content
1 bunch	scallions
3-1/2 oz. (100g)	Bergkäse, grated
4 tsp. (20g)	pumpkin seed, finely chopped
1 cup (250ml)	milk
2	eggs
1-1/4 cup (150g)	flour
	salt and pepper
	chili powder
	rapeseed oil

Preparation

■ Squeeze the juice out of the sauerkraut well and coarsely chop. Clean the scallions and cut into fine rings.

■ First, mix the milk, eggs, and flour well, and then mix in the sauerkraut, scallions, cheese, and pumpkin seeds. Season with the salt, pepper, and chili powder. Let everything soak for at least 15 minutes.

■ Form pancakes with a tablespoon and fry at low heat in portions in a pan in a lot of oil until both sides are nicely browned.

Ingredients (serves 8)

8	potatoes, waxy, for example Marabel
7 oz. (200g)	scamorza
3 tbsp. (40g)	Parmesan
1 bunch	chives
6 tbsp	whipped cream
1/4 cup (40g)	soft butter
2 tbsp.	coarse Dijon mustard
	salt
	pepper

Preparation

■ Wash the potatoes and wrap in aluminum foil. Based on the variety, cook on the grill at 480°F (250°C) for approximately 3/4 to 1 hour until the they are soft (fork test).

■ Remove the potatoes from the foil and grill for an additional 10 minutes.

■ In the meantime, cut the scamorza into fine cubes, finely grate the Parmesan, and cut the chives into small rolls.

■ Halve the potatoes and let cool.

■ Carefully remove the center of the potatoes with a spoon and make sure that the skin remains undamaged. Leave an edge of approximately 3/8" (1cm).

■ Mash the removed portion of potatoes well and stir with cream, butter, mustard, and Parmesan until a smooth mixture develops. This works well with the dough hook on a hand-mixer.

■ Fold in the scamorza cubes and chives. Season with salt and pepper.

■ Fill the potato mixture into the potato skins and grill on the grill grate for 10 to 15 minutes until crispy **(1)**.

1

Tip

If you like more melted cheese, you can replace 3-1/2 oz. (100g) of scamorza with Bergkäse. If you like it milder, mozzarella is a good alternative.

SIDE DISHES

193

Egg Noodles (Spaetzle) with Beans

The linguistic origin of spaetzle is highly disputed. Even before spaetzle was scraped from the board or pressed through a colander, the housewife formed small pieces of dough by hand or later with a spoon and placed them into boiling water. The dough in hand was associated with a sparrow; as a result, first the spaetzle was called "sparrows" — and was correspondingly bigger. Despite the linguistic uncertainty, spaetzle looks back at a history that began in the first half of the last century, as it was inexpensive to make, versatile, and nutritious.

Ingredients (serves 4-6)

1 lb. (500g)	beans
10-1/2 oz. (300g)	bacon
1 quart	water, hot
1 lb. (500g)	flour
4	eggs
1 tsp.	salt
	nutmeg
1/2 cup	water

Preparation

■ Remove the tips of the beans on both sides and cut the beans into 3/4" to 1" long (2-3cm) pieces. Remove the rind from the bacon and dice. Put the ingredients in the Dutch oven and pour water on top until everything is covered. For a 10" oven, this is exactly 1 liter.

■ Only with a lot of top and bottom heat cook for at least 20 minutes. The bite test determines whether the beans have to be cooked somewhat longer.

■ For the noodles, form a smooth dough from flour, eggs, salt, nutmeg, and water by kneading for five minutes and let this rest for 15 minutes.

■ Meanwhile, in a large pot, bring salted water to a boil. To prepare the spaetzle/noodles, you only need one tool: the spaetzle grater. The spaetzle grater basically looks like a cheese grater with a slide on top and functions as such. Fill the slide with some dough, place the spaetzle grater on to the edge of the pot, and move the slide back and forth while constantly pressing in the dough; the noodles fall on its own into the pot.

■ Cook the spaetzle/noodles in portions for 1 to 2 minutes and then skim off in a sieve. Repeat this process approximately three times until the dough is used up.

■ Put the still warm spaetzle/noodles into the oven, season lightly with pepper, and mix into the bean-bacon mixture. Cook again for 5 to 10 minutes with a closed lid. The noodles should have nearly entirely absorbed the liquid so that a thick stew has formed.

■ The hefty, but not too powerful, dish is served in soup dishes and tastes especially good when warm.

Spicy Grilled **Fries**

Ingredients (serves 4)

2	potatoes, waxy
2 tsp.	olive oil
1 tsp.	lemon juice
	seasoning blend for French fries

Preparation

■ Wash the potatoes and cut into fries.

■ Combine the potatoes with olive oil and lemon juice.

■ Grill the fries over direct medium heat with a closed lid for approximately 10 to 12 minutes until they are soft and brown. Turn the fries twice.

■ Sprinkle the fries with the seasoning blend and serve hot.

Tortilla Chips with Bell Peppers and Ground Meat

Ingredients (serves 20)

1/2	red pepper
1/2	yellow pepper
3 tbsp.	olive oil
7 oz. (200g)	ground meat, half pork, half beef
1 tbsp.	tomato paste
	salt
	black pepper
1 tsp.	paprika powder, sweet
3-1/2 oz. (100g)	Emmentaler cheese
20	tortilla chips

Preparation

■ Finely dice the peppers and brown in olive oil in a pan or wok. Add the ground meat and likewise brown until crisp.

■ Stir the tomato paste into the pepper-ground meat mixture and season with salt, pepper, and paprika powder. Let the mixture cool.

■ Finely dice the cheese and fold in.

■ Spread the ground meat-cheese mixture onto the tortilla chips and grill indirectly at medium heat until the cheese has melted.

Ingredients (serves 4)

2	eggplants
1/2	lemon
1 tsp.	salt
	spiced oil
2	garlic cloves
2 tbsp.	green pepper, from a jar
6 tbsp.	olive oil
2 tbsp.	thyme
1 pinch	black pepper

Preparation

■ Wash the eggplants, dry off, and halve lengthwise. With a sharp knife, cut an approximately 3/4" deep (2cm) diamond pattern into the surface. Coat the cut surfaces with lemon juice so that they don't turn dark, season with salt, and place on the grate with the cut surfaces down. Due to the salt, the eggplants lose a lot of water after approximately 30 minutes and taste better grilled.

■ Peel the garlic cloves and mince. Cut the green pepper into small pieces. Mix the olive oil with the garlic pieces, green pepper, thyme, salt, and black pepper.

■ Drizzle the seasoned oil onto the cut surfaces of the eggplants. Place the eggplants on the grate with the cut surfaces up and cook with indirect heat for 15 minutes.

■ Turn once and place directly on the charcoal so that the eggplants get a little more color.

Ingredients (serves 4-6)

27 oz. (750 g)	rice (3 pouches)
2	onions
1/2	bell pepper
2 tbsp.	tomato paste
1 tbsp.	paprika powder
	salt
	pepper
2 cups (500ml)	meat or chicken broth
1	chili
5 oz. (150g)	peas, frozen

Preparation

■ Put the rice in the oven **(1)**.

■ Peel the onions and finely chop. Seed the pepper and dice. Place everything with the paprika powder and meat broth in the oven and season with salt and pepper **(2)**.

■ Stir well and cook for 30 minutes with a lot of top heat. Before the end of cooking time, try the rice to see if it is done **(3)**.

Tarte Flambé

Ingredients (serves 4)

Dough

4 cups (500g)	flour
2 cakes (40g)	fresh yeast
3 tbsp.	milk, lukewarm
1 tsp.	sugar
1 tsp.	salt
4 tbsp.	oil
2 to 2-1/2 qts	water

Topping

1/2 lb. (200g)	bacon
3	onions
2/3 cup (150ml)	crème fraîche
7 oz. (200g)	cheese, grated
	pepper
	salt
	nutmeg

Preparation

■ Make a thin, uniform dough from the yeast, milk, and sugar. Mix in the flour, salt, and oil with a dough hook or food processor. Now, slowly add water until the dough loosens from the bowl (and fingers), but still feels moist.

■ Form the dough into a ball, sprinkle with flour, and, covered with a hand towel, let rise for approximately 1 hour. The rise time depends on the temperature. If, for example, it is placed in a heated kitchen on a high cabinet, 30 to 40 minutes is sufficient. The volume of the dough should have doubled at the end of rise time. Generally, the dough should rise for a longer amount of time rather than shorter.

■ For the topping, dice the bacon, cut the onions into fine rings, and grate the cheese. Stir the crème fraîche until fluid and season with a generous amount of pepper and nutmeg, but only a little salt.

■ Divide the dough into two portions. Lightly flour one dough ball, briefly knead by hand, and then on a floured surface roll out thin to the size of the tarte flambé (diameter approximately 11" [28cm]).

■ Place the dough onto a floured baking sheet and, as the base, spread on the crème fraîche. Spread the bacon, onions, and cheese on top.

■ Cook the tarte flambé in the wood-fired oven. Keep the door of the fire chamber closed, but the cooking chamber open. After approximately 2 minutes, when the bottom of the tarte flambé is done, open the door of the fire chamber so that the flames brown the dough. This process lasts approximately 30 seconds. The tarte flambé is finished when it is well browned.

Tip

The second half of the dough can be stored in the refrigerator for 10 to 14 days. During this time, the dough matures some and the base becomes even more savory.

Tarte Flambé **Variations**

Mexican Tarte Flambé
Base: Crème fraîche and coarsely ground pepper.
- Brown ground meat with chili and taco seasoning, add hot taco sauce and corn, and according to preference jalapeños and some grated cheese.

Greek Tarte Flambé
Base: Crème fraîche with multi-colored pepper.
- According to preference, top with tomatoes, diced sheep milk's cheese, olives, fresh basil, and some balsamic cream.

Asparagus Tarte Flambé
Base: Hollandaise sauce.
- According to preference, top with white and green asparagus, Parma ham, fresh chives, and some grated cheese.

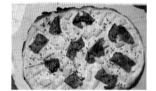

Pizza Tarte Flambé
Base: Tomato sauce with oregano.
- Top with cooked ham, salami, mushrooms, and a generous amount of grated cheese and sprinkle with pizza seasoning.

Hot Chili Tarte Flambé
Base: Crème fraîche with chili sauce.
- Top with tomatoes, salami, jalapeños, and small, red chili peppers and season with hot chili powder and some fresh chives.

Banana Tarte Flambé
Base: Créme fraîche.
- This "sweet and delicious" tarte is topped with bananas, Nutella, sugar, and cinnamon, and then slowly caramelized.

Cherry Tarte Flambé
Base: Crème fraîche
- Top with morello cherries, Nutella, sugar, and cinnamon and serve hot with a scoop of vanilla ice cream.

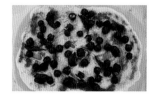

Ingredients (serves 4)

1	cauliflower
1	small zucchini
14 oz. (400g)	ground meat
1 bunch	scallions
2 tbsp.	tomato paste
1 cup	broth
1-1/2 oz.	white wine (Retsina)
8 oz.	sour cream
7 oz. (200g)	gratin cheese, grated
3-1/2 oz. (100g)	sheep milk's cheese
	baguette
	salt
	pepper

Preparation

■ Wash the cauliflower, divide into florets, and blanch in salt water for 6 to 8 minutes.

■ Cut the zucchini in half lengthwise and cut into thin, half-moon slices. Cut the sheep milk's cheese into small cubes.

■ Brown the ground meat with some olive oil in a pan. Meanwhile, cut the scallions into little rolls and then add to the ground meat and braise together. Add the white wine.

■ Mix the broth with the tomato paste and add to the ground meat. Combine everything well. Add the sour cream, stir well once more, and briefly boil down.

■ Place the cauliflower in the oven. First layer the zucchini on top and then the sheep milk's cheese. Pour in the meat sauce; make sure that the cauliflower florets and the zucchini are covered well.

■ Season with salt, pepper, and some nutmeg, and then sprinkle with gratin cheese.

■ After 45 minutes, and with a lot of top heat, the Mediterranean gratin is done.

Grilled **Tomatoes**

Ingredients (serves 5)

5	tomatoes
1 tbsp.	thyme
1 tbsp.	oregano
1	garlic clove
1 tbsp.	basil
1	scallion
2 tbsp.	olive oil
1/2 lb. (250g)	mozzarella
	salt
	pepper

Preparation

■ Cut off the top of the tomatoes and, at the bottom, remove a 1/16" thick (1-2mm) slice so that the tomato stands securely. However, do not remove too much at the bottom — you want the tomatoes stay thick. Keep the top.

■ Hollow out the tomatoes and then prepare the filling **(1)**.

■ Dice the mozzarella, crush the garlic, and cut the scallion into thin rings. Place with thyme, oregano, basil, and olive oil in a bowl and mix. Season with some salt and pepper **(2)**.

■ Using a spoon, put the mixture in the hollowed-out tomatoes and place the top back on top **(3)**.

■ Cook for 15 minutes with indirect heat in the kettle grill.

■ Carefully take out the tomatoes with a metal turner because they become quite soft.

Honey **Onions**

Ingredients (serves 6)

6	onions
1 tbsp.	butter
1 tsp.	turmeric
	pepper
	salt
8 tbsp.	honey
2 tbsp.	vinegar

Preparation

■ Melt the butter, stir in the turmeric, pepper, salt, honey, and vinegar, and briefly heat until all of the ingredients are blended.

■ Peel the onions and individually place on aluminum foil squares. The side length depends on the size of the onion. Form the square into a little sack that is open at the top **(1)**.

■ Carefully pour the butter mixture into the aluminum sacks.

■ Seal the sacks and grill for approximately 20 minutes **(2)**.

■ Unwrap the onions, sprinkle with salt, and serve hot **(3)**.

Ingredients (serves 4)

2 lbs. (1kg)	potatoes
1 cup (300ml)	cream
	salt
	pepper
	nutmeg
3	large onions
1 bag	cheese

Preparation

■ Boil the potatoes, rinse with cool water, and peel.

■ Cut the potatoes into evenly-sized slices using an egg slicer and place a layer in the oiled oven.

■ Finely dice the onions and add onto the potato layer. Season with salt and pepper, add the grated nutmeg on top, and add the cheese. Now begin with a new layer.

■ Proceed until the oven is almost full. For the last layer, put the cheese directly on top of the potato layer and season once more. The onions would otherwise burn because of the high top heat.

■ Pour the cream on top and close the lid of the oven.

■ Cook for approximately 30 minutes with a lot of top heat and little bottom heat.

■ As a variation, you can also add bacon, ham, or anchovies.

Cuban **Rice** Pot

Ingredients (serves 4)

1 can	corn
2 boil-in-the-bag	rice
7 oz. (200g)	ham
1/2 tsp.	saffron
	salt
	pepper
1	garlic clove
1/2	bell pepper
1 can	tomatoes
1	onion
2 tbsp.	parsley
1 liter	meat broth or chicken stock

Preparation

■ Cut open the rice pouch and put the rice in the oven. Dice the ham, pepper, and onion, crush the garlic, coarsely chop the tomatoes, and add everything to the rice. Mix in the saffron threads and combine everything well. Pour the chicken stock on top and stir again.

■ Heat for 30 minutes at high top heat until the liquid is completely absorbed by the rice.

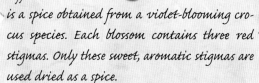

Saffron is a spice obtained from a violet-blooming crocus species. Each blossom contains three red stigmas. Only these sweet, aromatic stigmas are used dried as a spice.

Saffron is considered one of the most expensive spices of the world. It is grown in Iran and Europe, especially in the Mediterranean. Today imitation saffron is widely spread; therefore, you should never buy it ground — it is possible to just get an overpriced turmeric mixture.

Noodle Casserole

Ingredients (serves 4)

1 lb. (500g)	noodles, for example Fusilli
4	eggs
2	onions
1 cup	cream
2	zucchinis
2	cheese sausages (or similar sausages, such as Wiener, Schübling, or Lyoner)
1/2 lb. (250g)	gratin cheese
	nutmeg, freshly ground
	pepper
	salt

Preparation

■ Cook the noodles so that they are still somewhat firm to the bite. Oil the oven. Dice the onions and cut the zucchini in half lengthwise, and cut into slices. Quarter the cheese sausages.

■ Fill the oven in layers: first the noodles, then the onions, the zucchini on top of that, then add on the sausages, and finally spread a generous layer of cheese on top. With a 12" oven, you get two layers with the ingredients. Make sure that no onions are on top, otherwise they will burn (**1**).

■ Add the cream to the beaten eggs and whisk. Add the salt, pepper, and freshly grated nutmeg. As soon as the charcoal is lit, evenly pour in the cream-egg mixture into the oven (**2**).

■ Cover the lid with charcoal and place only 6 briquettes under the oven. With this, the casserole does not burn from below and will be nicely crispy on the top (**3**).

■ After approximately 45 minutes, the eggs are firm and the casserole is done.

Ingredients (serves 6)

1 packet	dry yeast
1 tbsp.	sourdough starter
1 tbsp.	sugar
1-1/2 cups (350ml)	water, lukewarm
4 cups (500g)	rye flour
3 tsp.	salt
1 tsp.	bread seasoning
	water for coating

Preparation

■ Mix the water and sourdough, and then dissolve sugar and salt in it. Add the flour and dry yeast and knead into a dough.

■ Cover the dough and let rise for 40 minutes in a warm place.

■ Knead the dough once again and let rise an additional 30 minutes in a bread mold.

■ Heat the wood-fired oven to 800°F (430°C). After you have maintained this temperature for 45 minutes, close the flue damper, clear the heat source from the baking chamber, test the stone temperature (flour or semolina test), and possibly cool down the stones.

■ Place the bread in the oven. Immediately, you will need to create a high humidity. To achieve this, you place a water container in the baking chamber and sprinkle the bread with water.

■ Turn the bread 180 degrees after 15 minutes. After approximately 30 to 40 minutes, test the doneness with a knock test. For this, "knock" on the bottom side of the bread with your knuckles. The bread is done when a "hollow" sound can be heard when knocking.

Rosemary **Potatoes**

This side dish is very easy to prepare and is always successful. Just from the smell of it, you feel like you're in Italy!

Ingredients (serves 4)

2 lbs. (1kg)	potatoes
2	garlic cloves
7 tbsp.	olive oil
3 sprigs	rosemary
	salt
	pepper

Preparation

- In a bowl, combine the olive oil, chopped rosemary, and crushed garlic cloves.

- Peel the potatoes, cut into cubes, and place raw in the oven.

- Pour the salt, pepper, and oil mixture on top and mix well once more.

- Cook for 60 minutes with a lot of top heat; after 30 minutes, stir once again with a metal turner.

Tzatziki

Ingredients (serves 4)

1	onion
1/4	cucumber
1/2 lb. (250g)	low-fat cottage cheese
8 oz. (227g)	crème fraîche
2	garlic cloves
1 tbsp.	olive oil
3-1/2 tbsp. (50g)	sheep milk's cheese
1 tbsp.	lemon juice
	salt
	pepper

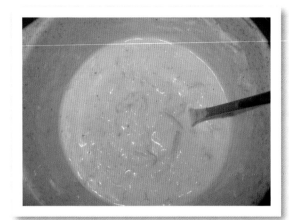

Preparation

■ Peel the cucumber and onion, mix the cottage cheese and crème fraîche.

■ Peel the garlic cloves and, together with the onion and sheep milk's cheese, grate into the cottage cheese mixture with a fine grater so that you can mix the ingredients.

■ Cut up the cucumber with a coarser grater so that a few larger firm pieces are in the dip.

■ Season with salt, pepper, and lemon juice. (If it's possible, marinate overnight.)

■ You can freeze the rest well in portions.

Dessert

Pineapple with Almond Pesto

Ingredients (serves 4)

1/2 cup (75g)	almonds with skin
1/2 container	lemon balm
2-3 tbsp.	brown sugar
2 tbsp.	rum
1 tsp.	sambal oelek (chili paste)
2 tbsp.	nut oil
4	pineapple slices, fresh
2 tbsp.	butter

Preparation

■ Roast and coarsely chop the almonds.

■ Chop the lemon balm leaves and mix with sugar, rum, sambal oelek, and oil. Mix in the almonds.

■ Coat the pineapple slices with butter and grill both sides for 2 to 3 minutes until they have a nice branding.

■ Cut the pineapples into small pieces and serve with the pesto.

■ A scoop of vanilla ice cream goes well with this.

Bananas with Orange Caramel

Ingredients (serves 6)

6	bananas
6 tbsp.	sugar
2 tbsp.	coconut or almond flakes
	fine orange zest
	juice from an orange

Preparation

■ At moderate heat, caramelize the sugar in a pan until it has a golden color, and then grate and stir in the citrus zest. Let the sugar solidify on parchment paper.

■ Finely chop the solidified sugar with a mortar or a large knife.

■ Cut the unpeeled bananas in half lengthwise and sprinkle with some orange juice, and then amply cover the bananas with the caramel powder.

■ Grill with direct heat for 5 to 7 minutes until the sugar has melted.

■ Vanilla cream, ice cream, or flavored cream goes well with this.

Tip
The grilling time and temperature depends on the condition of the bananas: the softer they are, the less time at a reduced temperature is necessary.

Pear Tart

Ingredients (serves 4)

4 slices	puff pastry
2	firm pears (for example Abate)
1 tbsp. (15ml)	Williams Christ fruit brandy
3-1/2 tbsp.	marzipan (50g)
5 tsp. (25g)	walnuts or roasted almonds, finely chopped
	dry white wine (Riesling)
	water
	sugar
	cinnamon
	apricot marmalade

Preparation

■ Peel the pears, halve, and remove the core.

■ Cook the pear halves in a water, sugar, white wine stock for 10 minutes until soft, and then let cool and pat dry.

■ Knead the marzipan together with the walnuts and fruit brandy. Form 4 even balls from the mixture and place them in the spot of the removed core.

■ Cut out 4 circles from the puff pastry. The diameter should be approximately 3/4" (2cm) larger than the length of the pear. Place each of the pear halves in the center of the circle with the cut surface down.

■ Score the dough around the pear.

■ Cut slices lengthwise into the pears and slightly fan out and sprinkle with sugar and cinnamon.

■ Cook on parchment paper on a stone at 650°F (350°C) for 5–6 minutes.

■ Spread the puffed edges of the dough thinly with some apricot marmalade and serve the tarts hot.

■ For garnishing, vanilla sauce, roasted almonds, and pistachio slivers are suitable. A mint leaf can also replace the pear stem.

Ingredients (serves 4)

4	apples, preferably red (for example, Braeburn)
1	lemon or lime

Filling

5 oz. (150ml)	apricot jam
5 oz. (150ml)	raisins
3 tbsp.	Calvados
1/2 tsp.	allspice, ground
1 pinch	cardamom
4 tsp.	butter
3-1/2 tbsp.	marzipan paste (50g)
6 tbsp.	almonds, sliced

Topping

4 tbsp.	double cream, 42% fat
	maple syrup
	Calvados
	pistachios, chopped
	powdered sugar
	cinnamon

Preparation

■ Remove the apple stem and blossom and place the apple on the stem end. Cut out the core in such a way that a base remains.

■ Score apple peel at the "equator" crosswise with a knife and peel the top side, or rather the blossom end **(1)**.

■ Brush all cut surfaces with lemon juice because otherwise they will become brown.

■ Roast the almond slices and set aside half.

■ Mix the other half of the almonds with the apricot jam, raisins, Calvados, allspice, cardamom, and marzipan until the marzipan has nearly entirely dissolved.

■ Fill the mixture into the apples without any hollow spaces and add a teaspoon of butter on each opening **(2)**.

■ Wrap each apple individually in aluminum foil and seal as tightly as possible.

■ Indirectly grill at approximately 390°F (200°C) for approximately 30 minutes until the apples are soft (pressure test).

■ Carefully lift from the foil onto a plate and pour the juice from the foil on top.

■ Season the double cream with maple syrup and calvados and place one tablespoon of the cream on top of each hot apple so that it melts over the hot apple.

■ Sprinkle with the remaining roasted almonds and garnish with powdered sugar, cinnamon, and pistachios.

Sweet Yeast **Dumplings**

Ingredients (serves 4)

1 packet	fresh yeast
5 tbsp.	milk
4 cups (500g)	flour
	salt
2-1/2 tbsp. (30g)	sugar
2 tbsp. (30g)	butter, warm
1	egg
1 cup (250ml)	milk, lukewarm
1 cup (250ml)	water
1 tbsp.	oil
1 bottle	wheat beer

Preparation

■ Mix the yeast with 1 teaspoon of sugar and 5 tablespoons of lukewarm milk and let rise for approximately 5 minutes until bubbles form.

■ Mix the flour with a pinch of salt, the remaining sugar, butter, and egg.

■ Pour the yeast solution over the dough. While kneading, pour on only as much lukewarm milk as needed so that the yeast dough easily loosens from the edge of the bowl. Let the dough rise for approximately 30 minutes in a warm area.

■ Form 6 balls from the dough.

■ Fill the water into the Dutch oven and mix well with 1 tablespoon of oil and 2 tablespoons of salt. Carefully place the sweet yeast dumplings next to each other **(1)**.

■ Heat the wood-fired oven to 480°F (250°C). Bake the sweet yeast dumplings at this temperature until the water has evaporated **(2)**.

■ During this time, open the wheat beer, pour some, and slowly drink while the sweet yeast dumplings bake.

■ Turn the Dutch oven in the wood-fired oven 180 degrees and continue baking for approximately 5 more minutes.

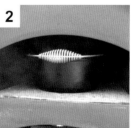

Exotic **Fruit Strudel** with Pomegranate and Mango Cream

Ingredients (serves 5)

10	strudel sheets, approximately 6" x 8" (15x20cm)
10	lychees
8	dates
1/2	pineapple
1	pomegranate
	powdered sugar
	green pistachios
	coconut syrup
8	ladyfingers
1-1/2 oz. (40g)	marzipan
	butter
	lime juice
2 cans	mangos
1-1/2 tbsp (2cl)	Cachaça (white rum)
3 tbsp (4cl)	lime juice
3-1/2 tbsp. (50g)	cream

Preparation

■ Cut the lychees, dates, and pineapple into small cubes of approximately 1/4" (5mm) edge length.

■ Crush the ladyfingers with a mortar and add.

■ Chop up the marzipan and also mix in.

■ Remove the seeds from the pomegranate, sieve, and season the seeds with powdered sugar, some lime juice, and coconut syrup.

■ Chop the pistachios and briefly roast, but they should not lose their color.

■ Spread liquid butter on the strudel sheets and place 2 sheets each on top of each other. Add 2 tablespoons of the marzipan mixture on top and roll up the sheets. Seal the ends.

■ Spread butter on the strudel, sprinkle the powdered sugar on top, and grill for 10 minutes at 360°F (180°C).

■ Dress with the pomegranate seeds and pistachios.

■ To make the mango cream, put the mango with the white rum and lime juice in a high container and puree. Now, strain through a fine sieve.

■ Mix well with the cream, put into a CO_2 cream dispenser, and squirt directly on the plate.

Fried Ricotta

Ingredients (serves 4)

5 oz. (150g)	ricotta
3 tbsp.	acacia honey (or another liquid honey)
1	egg yolk
3-1/2 oz. (100g)	blueberries
1 pinch	cinnamon
2	strudel sheets, approximately 15" x 12" (40x30cm)
5 tsp. (25g)	butter
1 tbsp.	Sichuan pepper
1/4 cup (50ml)	orange juice (approximately 1 orange)
1	lime, juice
1/2	lime, peel
	powdered sugar

Preparation

■ Drain the ricotta well, and then mix with 1 tablespoon of honey, the egg yolk, cinnamon, and the blueberries.

■ Grind the Sichuan pepper in a mortar and mix with the citrus juices, 2 tablespoons of honey, and lime zest.

■ Brush the strudel dough with the melted butter and cut into squares of approximately 4" x 4" (10x10cm).

■ Place 3 squares each on top of each other, twisting so that a star is formed. Carefully press the star into a greased muffin pan.

■ Add the ricotta filling into the depression and then bake in a pre-heated oven for approximately 10 minutes at 390°F (200°C).

■ Remove from the pan, sprinkle with powdered sugar, and serve with the sauce.

Ingredients (serves 4)

2   oranges
brown sugar
cinnamon
rum
cream, whipped
chocolate flakes
vanilla ice cream
aluminum foil

Preparation

- Peel the oranges with a knife, cut into slices, and seed.

- Fold the aluminum foil once so that you get a double layer.

- On the aluminum foil arrange the orange slices, beginning with the largest, so that half a fruit is formed again. Add some brown sugar with cinnamon between each layer.

- Drizzle a shot of rum on top and seal the aluminum foil to form a little sack.

- Cook on the grill for approximately 20 minutes at 390°F (200°C).

- Unwrap the oranges, spread on a plate, and garnish with cream, vanilla ice cream, and chocolate flakes.

Nut Wedges

Ingredients (serves 6)

Dough

2-1/2 cups (300g)	flour
2/3 cup (150g)	butter
6 tbsp. (75g)	sugar
1	egg

Coating

1 small jar	apricot marmalade
10-1/2 oz. (300g)	hazelnuts, coarsely ground
2/3 cup (150g)	butter
8 tbsp. (100g)	sugar
4 tbsp.	water
1 packet	chocolate frosting

Preparation

■ Knead the flour, butter, sugar, and egg into a dough. Roll out the dough on a baking sheet and poke with a fork.

■ Spread the apricot marmalade on the dough.

■ Bring the butter with sugar and water to a boil, add the nuts, and briefly cook together.

■ Distribute the mixture evenly on the dough and carefully spread. In the process the marmalade should remain under the nut mixture.

■ Bake with indirect heat on the grill at 430°F (220°C) for 20-30 minutes.

■ Immediately after baking, cut the nut wedges into triangles and let cool.

■ Melt the chocolate coating in a double boiler. Dip the pointed corners of the nut wedges into the chocolate and let cool.

Ingredients (serves 6)

Roquefort peach _____

6	peaches
24	thyme sprigs
12 slices	blue cheese
	brown cane sugar
	lemon juice

Espuma _____

2 cans	mangos
2/3 oz. (2cl)	Cachaça (sugarcane schnapps)
1-1/3 oz. (4cl)	lime juice
3-1/2 tbsp. (50g)	ProEspuma

Preparation

■ Halve and pit the peaches, and then sprinkle the cut surfaces with some lemon juice and then sugar.

■ Place each peach halve with the cut edge up on a piece of aluminum foil. For each, place 1 slice of cheese and a thyme sprig on top and wrap tightly in the aluminum foil.

■ Indirectly grill each pack for 30 minutes at 360-390°F (180-200°C).

■ Open the aluminum foil of the peach packs and replace the grilled thyme sprig with a fresh one.

■ For the Espuma, put the mangos, sugarcane schnapps, and lime juice in a tall bowl, puree, and strain with a fine sieve.

■ Combine the mixture well with ProEspuma, put into a CO_2 cream dispenser, and squirt directly on the plate

Roquefort Peach with Chocolate Cream and Chocolate Pudding Cake

Ingredients (serves 6)

Roquefort Peach

6	peaches
24	thyme sprigs
12 slices	blue cheese
	brown cane sugar
	lemon juice

Chocolate pudding cake

10-1/2 oz. (300g)	chocolate (70% cocoa)
1-1/3 cup (300g)	soft butter
2-1/4 cups (450g)	sugar
9	eggs
1 cup (120g)	flour

White chocolate cream

12	thyme sprigs
	leaves from 3 thyme sprigs
1 cup (225g)	whipped cream
9-1/2 oz. (270g)	white chocolate coating
2/3 cup (150g)	cream cheese
	egg white
	sugar

Preparation

■ Halve and pit the peaches, and then sprinkle the cut surfaces with some lemon juice and then sugar.

■ Place each peach halve with the cut edge up on a piece of aluminum foil. For each, place 1 slice of cheese and a thyme sprig on top and wrap tightly in the aluminum foil.

■ Indirectly grill each pack for 30 minutes at 360-390°F (180-200°C).

■ For the chocolate pudding cake, chop up the chocolate and melt with the butter at medium heat in a double boiler.

■ Beat the egg and sugar until frothy and combine with the chocolate mixture. The chocolate mixture must not be too hot so that the egg does not become firm.

■ Fold in the flour and fill the mixture into buttered and sugared molds and bake for 13 minutes at 390°F (200°C).

■ For the chocolate cream finely chop the thyme leaves and bring to a boil with the cream.

■ Grate the white chocolate, put in a bowl, and mix with the thyme cream to form a smooth mixture. Then mix in the cream cheese.

■ Put the cream into molds and let cool.

■ Pull the thyme sprigs first through egg white then through sugar and garnish the cream with it.

■ Open the aluminum foil of the peach packs and replace the grilled thyme sprig with a fresh one.

■ Serve each peach with chocolate pudding cake and a white chocolate cream.

Ingredients (serves 6)

1/2 lb. (250g)	soft butter
1 cup (210g)	sugar
1 packet	vanilla sugar
4	eggs
1/2 tsp.	salt
1 cup (125g)	flour, type 405
1 cup (125g)	cornstarch
1/2 tsp.	baking powder

Preparation

■ Stir the soft butter with the sugar and vanilla sugar until frothy. Add the eggs and salt and stir for at least 2 minutes.

■ Sift the flour and mix with cornstarch and baking powder. Slowly stir into the mixture.

■ Place the dough into a greased mold and bake for 45 minutes at 300°F (150°C) in the top compartment.

DESSERT

PART 3 Appendix

Index According to Grilling Method

Oven:

Rotisserie:

Dutch Oven:

Wood-Fired Oven:

Charcoal or Gas Grill:

Smoker:

Wok:

Index, Alphabetical

T

V

Ingredients

Preparation

Ingredients

Preparation

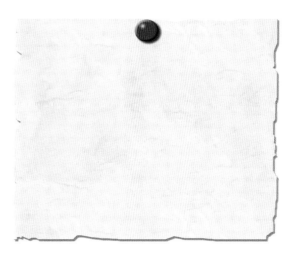

Ingredients

Preparation